"Ms. Kimbrell's book illustrate[s] us that it is possible to rise [above?] from the darkest depths of ad[diction? As a] counselor, this novel will pr[ovide those] who are in need of a good […]. Monks, and Mental Illness is also a great read. I had a difficult time putting it down until completion."

– Catherine Shane LPC, LCAS
Private Therapist

"This book gives a glimpse into the raw, naked, heart-wrenching world of addiction and the struggle to return from the depths of trauma and tragedy. Though fiction, it is a true-to-life example of one woman's journey from brokenness to picking up her own pieces, while trying to help others pick up theirs. This intriguing tale of self-medicating the torment of mental illness, takes place in the heart of the Western North Carolina recovery community."

– Vernetta Eleazer, MS, LCAS, CCS
Director: Swain Recovery Center

"This read is twisty, turny and very descriptive of how the disease of addiction lives and rages in the lives of everyday people and how life really does change for those who choose to "take the medicine" of recovery. The author has woven the language and steps of recovery into the life of characters, such as Becca. Becca comments:

> I tended to judge myself by who I thought [other people] were, based on how they looked and acted.

Becoming aware of how this type of judgment grips the psyche is very powerful and a psychic change can then occur. The author has strategically woven humanity and the 12 steps of recovery into a gripping, exciting story that was hard to put down."

– Victoria A. Lamberti, BA, OJT
Volunteer Program Services Coordinator
PEER Team Assistant Coordinator
Buncombe County Detention Facility

Drunks, Monks, and Mental Illness

DRUNKS, MONKS, AND MENTAL ILLNESS

...*based on a lie*

Barbara Willis Kimbrell

Grateful Steps
Asheville, North Carolina

Grateful Steps Foundation
Crest Mountain
30 Ben Lippen School Road #107
Asheville, North Carolina 28806

Copyright © 2017 by Barbara Willis Kimbrell
Library of Congress Control Number 2017951514
Kimbrell, Barbara Willis
Drunks, Monks and Mental Illness
. . . based on a lie

"Beriozka" lyrics, page 131, are determined to be in public domain.
"Little Bitty Tear" lyrics by Hank Cochran on page 203
is believed to be in public domain.
The cover photograph has been identified as not under copyright. The author has made every attempt to locate the owner of the item. Future printings of this book will include appropriate credit should new information becomes available.
The photograph of Rasputin on page xii has been identified
as not under copyright.

Author photo by Sabrina Kolton
ISBN 978-1-945714-14-6 Paperback

Printed in the United States of America
at Lightning Source

FIRST EDITION

All rights reserved. No part of this book
may be reproduced in any manner whatsoever
without written permission from the author.

www.gratefulsteps.org

For my grown children,
Nicole and Jacob, and all
those who were lost and
found their way or refused
to give up the search

Author's Note

This novel is, "twisty, turny," as one of the persons who reviewed my book dubbed it. That it is . . . for a reason. I wanted to portray the nature of addiction and mental illness, which tends to be a road with endless side roads, dead ends, hills and valleys. Without the recovery process—and yes, we can recover from a dual diagnosis—our lives are indeed chaotic.

I worked in the human service field for approximately twenty-five years and, like many of us in this field, encountered countless challenges myself in the battlefield of life. But sometimes, perhaps as a coping mechanism, I tended to deny the feelings associated with any past trauma just to get through the pain. This rejected trauma then rounded the corner, and sucker-punched me later in life. And my life, up until that encounter with trauma and for a period afterwards, tended to be reactive, filled with volatility, automatic and somewhat hasty. It is through evolving and becoming teachable, that my life has become more deliberate and mindful.

My earlier life emulated Rachel's. I seemed to always be flying "by the seat of my pants," and most times I forgot my pants. I never flew

Author's Note

for long. I usually crashed hard, running into treetops and getting tangled in the branches only to drop to the ground and get consumed by quick sand. Then, when I stopped struggling, and was about to let this quicksand take me under, I was granted the gift of surrender and recovery. I don't know exactly why or how it works, but I do know that I am grateful that I was given a reprieve. I can't help but cry for those, no longer among us, who didn't get an opportunity to choose recovery because they ran out of time and resources. It is my contention that many authors who write fiction have some of their own stories that seep into the pages like liquid fertilizer washing off a begonia. Rachel's father was Russian. My father was also Russian, and I relish my Russian heritage. It is the human condition to struggle. Like Rachel, I found solace in my spiritual journey, but it is a journey I have to recommit to on a daily basis.

Rasputin, a Russian monk, came from broken beginnings and chose his dark side until a spiritual mentor, whether because of fate or coincidence, took him under his charge and educated him. At first, Rasputin was able to draw from this strength and seemingly changed. However, over time, his intention and selfish motives appeared to win out, and he chose to succumb to his dark side, living a life of debauchery, which he tried to veil. He became a master manipulator and liar. Still, I'd like to believe that a part of him valued the spiritual principles to which he had been introduced.

He just lacked enough motivation, discipline, commitment and desire to stay the course.

I am grateful that I have found enough foresight to know that it could prove disastrous should I, too, forget this premise.

Barbara Willis Kimbrell

Acknowledgments

I thank Nicole and Jacob, from whom I may have learned more than they learned from me; Staci, her husband and my granddaughter; Hazel; my brothers and their wives; my "soul sister," Angie, who encouraged me to pursue my writing; my other family and friends who inspired me along the way; Cathy Mitchell for her skilled copy editing, my mother and father, who are gone but not forgotten; my grandmother; my friend Maija, who has since passed; and my dear partner, Joel, who restored my faith in love. Also, I want to dish out a huge ladle of thanks to my best friend, Catt, who stood by me even when I tried to push her away. But mostly to my Higher Power, who saved my life.

Rasputin

△

No matter where I go, there I am.
12 step program wisdom

"Your Demons are charming!" the dream voice whispers as I struggle to become awake. My eyes slowly open. First I wiggle my toes, and then I stretch my lower limbs. They are stiff as recycled plastic wood. My dog, Satchmo, part Boxer and part Jack Russell Terrier, hears my rousing, gets up on his hind legs, and sticks his muzzle in my ear. A half smile creeps onto my face.

Satchmo was rescued from "doggy death row." I adopted him from the Humane Society. He is white with a black circle around his right eye and a huge pumpkin-colored spot on his side. When I run my hand over the ridge of his back, I am sure to dislodge a puff of little white hairs. Still, I absently stroke his back as he stands—like a young child trying to drink from a water fountain on a hot summer day—and laps my face with his pink tongue. His tail had been cut off, called "docking the tail," which is purely cosmetic. I understood the original idea was to prevent the dog—especially a boxer who has little fur to cushion the blow should his tail get injured—from getting his tail caught in something. I seriously did not think his previous owner put much thought into it and probably felt it just looked "cool."

The shelter volunteer told me, "It was heartbreaking. The woman who brought him in said she saw a man pull over to the side of the road adjacent to her house, throw him out of the truck, and kick him several times before speeding away and leaving him for dead. "This man was about thirty-something," she said, "and kind of scruffy looking." This inhumane act was so brutal that she remembered the gun rack in the back window of his truck and his bumper sticker:

>IF YOU CAN READ THIS,
>YOU ARE FOLLOWING TOO CLOSE

The volunteer shook her head with disgust. Satchmo's brown eyes screamed, "Take me home and love me."

And I did. Satchmo from day one had a tendency to shake. I would whisper to him that everything would be okay, although I was never truly convinced. I sometimes plan out what I will do if I run into this man, but click off my imagination because indulging those negative feelings might throw my psyche out of balance and effect my unborn twins.

I reach behind me on our Tempur-Pedic mattress I insisted on buying, and my fingertips brush lightly against the slightly moist skin of my husband, Mike. A sigh escapes my lips, and any anxiety that might have surfaced diminishes.

We purchased the mattress during the Memorial Day Discount Super Duper Sale at Sears the week before. "It is really hard for me to get relaxed, and this mattress is so comfy," I said while I lounged as if I were posing for a commercial. I knew it was a luxury item, something my parents would have scoffed at, so I pressed harder. Mike grumbled about how much it cost, wrinkling his forehead as he always did when he thought he was going to have to hand over some cash.

"You don't have this appendage," I joked, gazing down at my pregnant, lopsided belly as one of the twins played handball against the left side of my stomach. I stuck out my lower lip to emphasize that he was partially responsible for my discomfort.

"Anything to please you, beautiful," he said. "She's the boss," he said as he turned to the salesman, who gladly added up the final cost and took Mike's credit card.

Manipulation still serves a purpose, I think. I breathe deeply, plucking at my past and stirring up emotions like a willow branch in murky lake water. But I quickly drop the branch for fear of what lurks beneath the glassy surface. I don't like the things I had done to get what I thought I wanted. I stooped to levels so low that even a slug wouldn't want to crawl on its underbelly.

Lying, manipulating others and fear are some things I am familiar with. I am an alcoholic and an addict. Thankfully, today, I am in recovery.

△

First things first.
12 step program wisdom

Trying not to move, I lay on the bottom mattress in my metal-frame bunk bed and stared at the springs above me. I usually tossed and turned like an old person with restless leg syndrome. But tonight I was careful not to move because the springs made a squeaking sound that might wake up my baby brother lying in his crib strategically placed by my bedroom door. My brother, Thomas, had colic. My mother was tired and cranky. I was four years old. I was terrified. I pulled the scratchy wool blanket up to my chin. It smelled like my father—a combination of cherry pipe tobacco and his distinct body odor—the essence of authority to me. It was his prized Texas A&M blanket he purchased during his undergraduate years. This was my first memory: fear coiled up in the pit of my stomach like my mattress springs.

I couldn't sleep. I woke up so scared that my insides danced like my mother and father when they had those "martini parties." Our neighbor, Mr. Redmon, was the villain in these dreams. His face was distorted and hideous. But it was his hands that terrified me the most. They were huge, filthy—with crud caked under his nails—and he always smelled like vomit.

In real life, he had dimples and curly sun-red hair. I thought he looked like a character out of the comics, which made him seem like someone you could trust. Mother asked him to babysit nights when she was going out. His wife had left him years ago, and he lived on a limited income, so I suppose the extra money came in handy. His promises of homemade cookies had already brought me to his house before he started coming to our house. He would play hide and go seek for a lot longer than any grownup I knew, and of course, I loved cookies.

"Call me Ollie," he said, his voice filling the room.

"Ollie . . . that's a funny name," I said, liking how the name rolled off my tongue. It's kinda like a clown's name."

"You're funny!" he said. He laughed as he tickled me. I relished the attention. Afterward, he pulled out an over-sized coloring book and big, thick crayons. I liked how they felt in my hands. We colored together, and he never criticized my color choice or that I colored outside the lines, and I loved to add little squiggles to the page. They were my "beauty bugs."

He let me cook with him. I made a mess, but he never seemed to mind. He always had a habit of getting right up behind me as I stirred the bowl.

He wrapped his arms around me and placed his hands on my little hands to help me stir. At first it didn't feel uncomfortable, but more like a down sleeping bag on a cold day. Hugs were something I didn't get much of in my house.

One day, before he started to come to our house to babysit, I was at his house. It was the weekend. Mother had been snapping at me like a pit bull on a tether.

"Rachel . . . I thought I told you to clean your room. You better have it picked up by the end of the day, or there will be no TV."

I promised I would clean it up. I then went to Ollie's house to play. Mother never commented on how peculiar it seemed for a grown man to take so much interest in me. She just wanted me out of her hair.

He tickled me. His big fingers dug into my arm pits at first. Then he tickled my belly, which was my giggle spot. His hands were playing me like a piano, but I didn't like the tune they were playing and began to wriggle my way out of his reach. In the middle of this play, he shot upright and looked at me with eyes kind of like my brother gets when he is fighting sleep.

"You wanna see something? It's kinda like a firecracker exploding," he said as he unzipped his pants.

My tummy turned sour like milk sitting too long on the stoop.

"I gotta go home and clean my room," I said.

"Aww . . . this won't take long, little girl." And it didn't, but I didn't like it.

When he started to come to the house to watch me and Thomas, he wanted me to make his firecracker explode and would not take no for an answer. He started touching me in places that I knew somehow he shouldn't and even though it kinda felt good, it made me cry.

One evening, just when the crickets started their serenade, he came into my room. I tried to curl up tight in the space between my bed and the wall, but he yanked me into the center of the bed. He put his thick rough finger like tree bark inside of me. It hurt and I squirmed, trying to get him to take it out.

"You like it, don't you, little girl?"

I cried harder, and the harder I cried, the more he panted like a thirsty dog.

I told him to stop and even bit him once when he tried to put his firecracker in me. That is when he hit me hard in the face with the back of his hand. My face stung worse than any bee sting I had ever had.

"You better not say anything to anyone, or you'll be sorry. I will break your little brother's neck."

I stopped crying.

He told my mother that I was running down the hall in my socked feet, even after he told me not to, fell, and collided with the corner of the door.

She looked at my discolored face and believed him. I hated her at that moment almost as much as I hated him.

It was then I started cutting off, from my waist down, the bottom half of any photographs my parents had of me.

My mother was too preoccupied with my brother to notice anything was wrong. In fact, if I woke Thomas up due to my restlessness, she became furious with me. She spent long evenings trying to get him to sleep and was exhausted and irritable. So I tried to bury this fear like a metal box filled with stolen money. My restless mood turned into irritability and then a thick sadness that quietly suffocated me.

I was jealous. My mother constantly worried about and tried to appease Thomas. It seemed to me that Mother spent all her time with him and had no time for me. I distinctly remembered Mother telling me that she didn't like "whiney little girls that cling to your fingers!" I felt lost, alone and confused.

* * *

We moved every time I sneezed. Although at times it felt disruptive, I certainly was relieved to have some distance between me and Ollie. My father was away from home for long periods of time; he was an officer in the Army. As my brother grew up, he didn't seem to want me around much either. Sometimes he became bored and terrorized me. Once, he dumped a whole pillowcase of daddy longlegs on me. He was four years younger, but seemed almost six inches taller from birth. He also seemed to succeed in life with no effort. He could add up numbers in his head and seemed a natural accountant. He saved up his allowance, made deals with the neighborhood kids selling baseball cards, had a paper route and always had money to spend. I lost money or bought gifts for people in exchange for friendship. His hair was fine, but thick, and it always seemed to fall into place without having to run a comb through it. I always had to tame my wavy locks and yet looked like Medusa. I always compared myself to Thomas, and I did not measure up. So, I kept my distance unless I was trying to get him in trouble. Thomas was cut from a different cloth in my mind's eye. He was expensive silk, and I was a cotton remnant.

In the cool of the evening, when I was alone and ready for bed, I stared at the springs of the bunk bed above me and fantasized. In my imagination I was the envy of everyone and admired by all. But most of all, I was fearless. It was a survival mechanism, but not as effective as drugs and alcohol.

△

Resentments are a luxury we can't afford.
12 step program wisdom

My mother found me exasperating. I drank. I did drugs. I was sexually promiscuous. I constantly found myself in trouble. Even though she had been made aware of some of the severe sexual abuse I had experienced as a child, she did not give it any credence. She did not seek outside help. Professional counseling might have helped us negotiate what had happened to me. I am not sure if she thought looking at it too closely would only magnify it while not looking at it would make it magically go away. I found out later she had been taught some equally confusing messages about intimacy and sexuality as a young girl. But of course, I was too focused on being a victim to absorb that anyone else, let alone my mother, could have also had been traumatized. And I was still a child.

"You are so incredibly stupid at times, Rachel!" she offhandedly remarked at the oddest of times and stormed off. There was no pattern of triggers that caused this reaction. If my father was in the room, he was left looking like a fish in an aquarium—mouth gaping open, eyes bulging. Then he pulled himself together and tried to comfort me with a joke, or a reassuring word. Occasionally he would put on one of his Russian records, and we listened quietly as my tears dried on my cheeks.

My mother yelling at me for no reason resulted in a lot of tension. At times it escalated into physical altercations between my parents. Other times, I was the brunt of both their anger. On one occasion, there had been a reason. Because I cursed at her, my mother whacked me upside the head with the hard-back book she had been reading. I think it was *Oliver Twist*. I spit in her face. My father retrieved a rubber hose and whipped me soundly. First I cursed and tried to run from him. He had to catch me. But catch me he did. "Stand still and take it like a man!" he barked out of habit, I suppose. "But I'm a girl!" I screeched back at him. In an act of defiance and *maybe* to make my father proud, I did my best to stand still as he administered my thrashing. I ended up with bruises on my backside as evidence. I just retreated further into myself.

I was the first of two children born to a handsome Russian immigrant and a dark-haired woman of English descent with good posture. My father described her as "unassuming" and "brilliant." He met her while attending the University of California at Berkley.

* * *

Whenever I thought of my father, I sighed. My father was my champion in this marathon called life. Even though he was hardly ever home due to work constraints, I always clamored for attention when I was young. And I pestered him unmercifully. He was not physically affectionate. Hugs were provided on a limited basis. But I knew he loved me. He was strict and set high standards for his children. I remember the comment he made the day he picked me up from jail after yet another one of my impulsive expeditions. He had a clear, deep voice that made me want to pee in my pants if I thought I had done something wrong. I knew he kept that short piece of a rubber hose in his drawer under his neatly rolled color-assorted socks, in case I misbehaved, as I had misbehaved on many an occasion.

"Nothing but drunks, monks and mental illness in our family," he said, as if this explained why he had to pick up his 13-year-old daughter from jail.

I had run away from home thinking I could recreate myself and maybe even join the Rainbow Family, a communal group of individuals who I thought lived the ultimate existence. I fancied myself a throwback to the hippie era. I liked the idea of living like a bohemian—where everyone was equal—dressed in a flowing skirt, pursuing my artistic side. Little clue did I have that I already had the disease of addiction setting up camp in my brain. Because of the effects of the excessive amounts of booze I had consumed, I ended up in a cold cell with no mattress in Fayetteville, North Carolina, an army town. Several vets donning long-haired wigs and I were picked up in a paddy wagon. The vets had been selling drugs to underage girls.

I always heard about people pacing in their cells on television. Now I was. I had counted how many footsteps it took to get from the door to my bunk and how many from my bunk to the single toilet that was attached to the wall and was constantly running. I could see into the other cell through the hard, cracked bars with initials scratched in them. An old, ashy black woman with a few bald patches on her head was moaning, talking to herself incessantly and sometimes yelling and punching into the air. After three days of eating cold eggs and grits and watching this older black woman in the cell next to me go through what the jailer identified as delirium tremens, the detective in my case finally convinced me to tell him who I was.

"These are the pictures of other runaways in the area who were found dead," he reported with a deadpan face as he pushed some worn photographs toward me. I glanced down at these faces of young girls—unknown to me—who could be anyone in my gym class. I cried. The thought of them never running up and down a basketball court or even being selected last for a team sport was a horror that grabbed my throat, and I couldn't catch my breath. I gladly confessed. I was tired of sleeping on an iron bunk with the assorted "church ladies" preaching to me periodically from the other side of the bars and the rank smell of vomit wafting up from the cell next to mine.

My father came to pick me up. Stone-faced, he made no comment other than about our family genealogy. I came out of lock-up clutching my beanbag tiger, which was a testimony to my age and maturity level. It was the only thing, other than a tattered night bag filled with a change of clothes, that I took with me when I hitchhiked across the state. Father must have decided when he saw me that there was no reason to reprimand me. He figured I had been punished enough for my indiscretions.

My brother, Thomas, on the other hand, seemed to do no wrong. He was like salt in my wounds. I always compared what I was feeling on the inside to how he appeared on the outside. And he looked like the Golden Child to me. He was a champion in sports and school. He was the quarterback on the football team and president of his class. Everyone, including my parents, couldn't get enough of him. I recall on one occasion, in one of my earlier childish attempts to bring about his demise, I had mixed up a wonderful concoction of creamy peanut butter, dirt and pieces of gravel and spread it in the sink. I told my mother that Thomas pooped in the sink. In my child mind, it seemed reasonable. It did not occur to me she would be able to figure out my scam. Of course it smelled like peanut butter, and my brother was not big enough to get up in the sink and squat, nor am I sure if the sink would hold him.

In the end, I was punished soundly for "making up stories" and was sent to my room with fresh bruises. The bruises were said by my mother to be a result of me not "standing still" not because she hit me too hard. I had bruises on my back and legs as well as my hind end. I added this incident to my list of resentments. I very seldom took responsibility for my part in any perceived wrong-doing. I always felt justified. It validated my conviction that I was either adopted or an alien left behind from another planet. I was different. And a part of me liked being sad, angry and unwanted.

***

Another time, when I was a little older, I was convinced that if I had a pair of ankle combat boots that all the older "cool kids" wore, I would fit in. I would be popular like Thomas. Thomas had been moved ahead one year in school because he was considered gifted. And because of his size, his athletic ability and bravado, he fit in easily. I was already having trouble at school at a young age, keeping friends due to my aggressive and erratic acting-out behavior. Other children's parents did not want their children to play with me. My mother did not think of the combat boots as particularly practical or "becoming" and refused to buy them. Besides, the ones I wanted were made of real leather and not cheap. So, I threw my "ugly shoes" away and told her that they had been stolen when I changed into my gym shoes. However, she just bought me another pair of almost the same kind.

I seethed with resentment. I went to Sears after school. The boots I wanted were actually in the men's section. I looked out of the corner of my eyes in both directions and quickly crammed one of the boots into my knapsack. I walked around nonchalantly pretending to be interested in other items on the shelves. I then returned to the second boot lying in its box, scooped it up, and shoved it hard into my sack. I quickly left the store. I hid the boots at the bottom of the hill. I changed into them before I got on the bus every morning and changed into the other shoes before I got home.

* * *

My mother tried time and time again to help me with my "crippling shyness." She enrolled me in the Girl Scouts.

"It'll be a good way to meet other kids and to learn the value of hard work. You have to earn merit badges. It should be fun."

She took classes at the local community college. She dropped me off en route to night school. I sat outside in the dark and did not go in. When she picked me up, I quickly jumped inside the car.

"Did you have a good time?"

"It was okay," I muttered. And that was the end of the conversation. She probably thought I was being my usual brooding self. I was trying not to get caught in a lie, and I guess I wanted to please her.

After a couple of weeks, the telephone rang, and I heard my mother's not-so-happy voice speaking into the receiver.

"She what? You mean she has not attended one of the meetings? But she brought back some merit badges, and I helped her with some of the requirements."

I darted into my room and sat in the dark.

She came in my room and flipped on the light.

"Why are you sitting here in the dark? And what the hell made you steal merit badges meant for some of the other girls. Why did you steal them out of the drawer Mrs. Collins kept them in? What is wrong with you? Are you stupid? Didn't you realize that you couldn't go on pretending you were going to these meetings? Again, I'm asking you what is wrong with you! Will you answer me?"

I looked down at my hands and didn't say a single word.

"Well, you will have to return those badges and apologize. And of course, we will take you out of the Girl Scouts. I don't think they give merit badges for thievery. You are grounded for two weeks, and that means no TV either!"

When I still didn't say anything, she came over and started shaking me.

"Will you say something? What is wrong with you? Oh, for God sake . . . you are infuriating!" She turned and walked off.

I stood up and turned the light back off, crept back into bed and fell asleep with my clothes still on.

If I hadn't been a child, maybe I would have realized that when she admonished me for being "stupid," perhaps she just meant what I was doing was stupid, not that *I* was stupid. But instead, I believed the words she recited and internalized it. I resigned myself to my belief that I was dumber than a roach crawling over a can of Raid and I stopped wanting to please her.

"You think I'm bad . . . I'll show you just what a bad ass I can be!" I said in an effort to console myself, as I licked the inside corner out of a baggie that once was filled with coke. Booze and drugs became my ally because I was convinced I didn't have one. That was until I met Maija.

Maija was more like a mother and mentor than a guardian. She had been in my life since I was 11. She had been the Guardian Ad Litem (GAL) assigned to my case. My school had called the Department of Social Services. It was reported that I might be a victim of both "inappropriate discipline" and emotional abuse after I had missed a week of classes and had come back to school with belt marks on my back, buttocks and legs and a bruise on my face where my mother had slapped me hard. I had made up a series of stories laced with some truth. I was a truant and did not respond well to boundaries or discipline. My nickname was "Wild Thing." Although that did not *excuse* my parents' harsh and anger-fueled discipline, it certainly did explain it. Either way, the allegations were substantiated and the Department of Social Services opened their case.

Maija was an angel with a briefcase. She actually listened to my emotional upheavals, allowed me to cry instead of belittling me when I did and saw some redeeming qualities buried under all my eat-shit-and-die stares. She tucked strands of unruly auburn hair behind my ear and whispered in an even, nurturing tone, "Rachel, you are beautiful."

It was clear to everyone else other than me, that I was an addict, and now that a collection of community human service workers, my "Henchmen" as I sneeringly called them, had become involved—including a juvenile justice service officer, a cognitive-behavior therapist and an intensive case manager—my behaviors and interactions with the world had become fodder for my treatment team. And all of them together, I was convinced, didn't possess half the tenderness and empathy that Maija did in her little toe.

My cognitive-behavior therapist scolded, "I understand your mother found a pipe in your sock drawer. You are an addict, Rachel. Do you think that is a way for you to rebuild trust?" She asked me this in a condescending tone, which I imagined Jesse Helms, a former North Carolina U.S. Senator, might have used when debating President Bill Clinton's decision to nominate an openly lesbian woman to the assistant secretary position in the Department of Housing and Urban Development. She used a tone similar to the one my mother used when she insinuated I didn't have a sharp enough mind to understand politics. Mother always followed up with some statement about how artistic I was and that I should pursue that avenue, as if that made up for her derogatory comment. I ended up feeling as if I were lacking somehow. I did watch the news and read the paper . . . when I wasn't getting high and when no one was watching or hovering over me to quiz me about what I had just seen. When Helms emphasized he wasn't going to put a lesbian in a position of authority, it felt comparable to my mother telling me I was not capable of understanding the world around me. I wasn't gay, as far as I knew, but I did feel discriminated against. And I was still uncertain about whether or not I was stupid.

"I thought the sock drawer was better than the kitchen table. Besides," I snapped, "seems to me she is violating my trust by snooping around where she doesn't belong," And then I said under my breath, but loud enough for her to hear, "Bitch."

"Young lady, it is no wonder you are having problems at school with an attitude like that. I've reviewed your standard test results, and you are unquestionably intelligent, but you sure can't tell it by your grades. I believe you can do so much better, Rachel." She droned on and on as she rifled through the papers on her lap, only occasionally looking at me. I stared at her shoes and decided right then and there I hated her. They were nondescript navy blue pumps and much too old for her, but exactly matched the suit she was wearing.

"Uh . . . think you can get a better wardrobe . . . fashion is something you obviously know nothing about!" I practically screamed trying to change the subject.

"I am going to court this afternoon," she said, "and I try to be respectful of this process. You could learn a thing or two from me." I made a mental note to do the opposite of anything she might suggest.

The year I turned 15, I was called to the assistant principal's office. I figured it must have been for some misdeed. As I walked down the hall with my head bent forward like someone had slapped me once too many times upside my head, I could still hear my father's voice saying, "Stand up straight, stomach in and chest out." But when I tried to walk tall, it felt like some invisible puppeteer was dictating my every move, and I would become hypervigilant. Quickly, instinctively, I would turn my head back toward the ground. Something about watching the forward movement of my feet felt comforting.

I stared at the discolored, worn linoleum. I was convinced it had to have been me who had worn down that linoleum, I had been to his office so many times. I opened the glass door to the central offices and headed my way back to the all-too-familiar room.

I nodded sourly at the staff congregated around the copy machine. They had been engaged in office gossip but looked away and busied themselves when I walked by.

I pushed open the door without knocking. Mr. Stewart looked up. His eyes were hooded by thick eyebrows, and he seemed more worried than stern. I sullenly plopped down on the plastic and aluminum chair in front of his desk.

"What did I do now?"

"Rachel, there has been a tragic accident. Your parents are dead."

I stared at him and could hear my breath as my chest rose and fell. I wondered if he could hear it.

***

It seemed surreal to me that my parents died so suddenly on a plane trip to Moscow. Both my father and mother loved Russian history. Once I was immersed in my addiction, I became oblivious to my heritage and showed no interest, and because I was behind in school and perhaps, because my parents didn't trust that I might not bolt while overseas, they left me behind. The plane crash killed them both instantly. There were some survivors, but my parents were not among those fortunate souls. I remember staring blankly at the television coverage, as if my essence had been on that plane with them. Fate is an odd thing. Luckily, the courts allowed Maija to take physical custody of me, and I moved in with her, her pug and a house filled with warmth and hope.

Both my parents before their deaths had sent me to counselors for treatment. So, of course, after their deaths, I continued in treatment, although an unwilling participant. Even though my parents did not seek out treatment for me until the Department of Social Services became involved and not earlier, when it might have actually helped after my sexual abuse, they eventually agreed to it because I was deemed incorrigible and they could not appropriately manage me.

Still, I have to give my parents credit: they participated, or at least showed up for family therapy and groups composed of other parents with "difficult" children. I remembered my father telling a bunch of his friends over dinner, with me sitting at the table, how he had challenged my therapist during one of the group sessions with other parents.

"One of the fathers kept droning on and on about how his daughter was eating too much, and I interrupted him. I asked him, rather loudly, what his daughter's eating habits had to do with my daughter filling her arm with cocaine. Then the therapist told me, 'That's good—emote, emote.' I turned to him and told him what he could do with his therapy group."

I almost melted into my chair when I felt all those adults' sympathetic eyes staring at me. I got up abruptly and knocked my chair over. I ran to the safety of my room. I could hear my father yell after me, but I didn't stop. I didn't want those strangers to see me cry. I never knew if my father came in later to check on me because I fell immediately asleep with the lights still on.

* * *

My parents, in hindsight, were probably as befuddled as I was. Raising an angry, defiant daughter who resisted authority no matter what the underlying motive might have been, was probably as hard as pulling every single weed out of an acre garden by hand. And, after their sudden death, I was no more in touch with my feelings than I was when they were alive.

Give time time.
12 step program wisdom

WHEN I REACHED my late twenties, I became even more preoccupied with my looks, if that was humanly possible. Every imperfection seemed like an insult. I noticed the fine lines around my eyes that probably no one else would notice. I repeatedly told myself that age didn't matter. Even though I wanted to think of myself as philosophically and spiritually more advanced, I believed I was shallow at the core. I obsessed about my looks and was vain, despite the fact I professed I wasn't. And I always had a man in my life, which validated my incessant need to feel beautiful.

My belief system seemed at war with itself. I had two pervading thoughts that rattled around in my head. One voice tried to knock me off my idealistic podium. "There is no real meaning in life." "You are not capable of creating anything substantial in this life." "You are a misfit." "You are damaged goods." These intruding thoughts unnerved me and made my bones ache.

My other voice almost crooned to me. This was my internal cheerleader. "You just need to do the next right thing." "People are essentially good." "Life is an adventure." "Faith can cure all things." I liked this voice best.

One nondescript morning, I shuffled to the kitchen in my socked feet and turned on the coffee. It had become a habit. I preferred the syrupy sweetness of a McDonald's Mocha Frappe. I thought of my boyfriend, Travis. Travis always harped on saving money, and I used to make coffee for him every morning. Sometimes, I would sneak and get my coffee at McDonald's whenever I thought I could get away with it. I couldn't bear to hear Travis harp on the negative side effects of preservatives. Travis thought the preservatives in McDonald's products would rot his vocal chords and destroy his singing voice. Then the reality of my situation slapped me in the face. Travis is dead!

Travis had been there to pick up the pieces after my marriage had fallen apart. I had married at the early age of 17. My marriage had lasted barely seven years.

When I first met Travis, he reminded me of a struggling country music star with his lean good looks, thick blue-black hair and deep, gruff voice. His wide-set blue eyes made him look so innocent. And he could sing the pants off even the most staunch woman libber! He became my obsession. I wanted to fix him. Being in a relationship, even a bad one, kept my mind off having to look at myself. Travis had no driver's license, recently got out of prison with an impressive criminal background and lived with his mother. It was not the Bates Motel, but his reliance on her was still creepy. The fact that we met at a 12 Step support group when neither of us had much clean time was of little significance to either of us. It was lust at first sight.

I knew that Travis was bad news, but I ignored my inner chidings. The few friends I had lectured me and sputtered and spewed about me being "codependent." I hated that label. I could easily rationalize and convince myself it was a term coined by a bunch of self-care group addicts who had nothing better to do than come up with explanations for self-inflicted behavior. I preferred being by myself most days. People, especially men, cannot be trusted. I told myself that I was neither dependent on anyone nor needed to hold onto a man just to avoid feelings of abandonment. This seemed like such "whiney-girl" behavior.

As I puttered around the house looking for something more appealing to do than what had to be done, I glared at the collage of pictures on the wall leading upstairs. A picture of Travis still hung on the wall.

Frantically, in a half-baked attempt to prove myself sane, I took his picture down and replaced it with a butterfly carved out of beeswax. It was a symbolic gesture of healing and a belief I would metamorphose. Satchmo sat at the bottom of the staircase and stared at me.

I poured a cup of coffee and went outside and perused my yard. I had sold the updated cottage-style house my husband and I had lived in for our entire marriage and bought an over-sized money pit. Actually, the house had vintage charm, character and great bones, but with almost two acres, it seemed overwhelming. I had bought it because I thought it would fit both Travis's and my needs, but I would never have purchased it for just myself. Now there was all this unfinished work that Travis, the "wanna-be contractor" who couldn't read a measuring tape when he was stoned out of his mind, had promised to fix. I still wanted to restore the home to its original splendor but had lost my motivation.

Travis had probably been stoned or thinking about getting stoned our entire relationship except maybe at the very beginning . . . so most everything he had said was a lie. I succinctly remembered looking out the window early on in our romance and seeing Travis sprawled out in the mulch he was supposed to be depositing around my plants, mouth slightly parted, with a piece of mulch almost lodged in it. *Aww . . . he must be tired.* Travis loved opiates, among other drugs. *What a dolt I had been!* My head ached as I looked at the surrounding yard where Travis and his ever-rotating band of hired misfits had thrown building material, random trash and cigarette butts. I almost vibrated with resentment.

Still, when I got the phone call I was surprised. Maybe being oblivious to what intuition is screaming is how denial disguises itself. The authorities had found Travis's lifeless body in a "dipsty"-dumpster with discarded pieces of drywall, bent nails and mounds of sawdust. When I identified the body, he still had what appeared to be sawdust in his nostrils . . . or cocaine, it was hard to tell.

* * *

As invariably happened, I started a trip back in my mind thinking maybe if I understood why I did what I did and continued to do, I might be able to repair myself. I recalled all my attempts to "fix myself" before I came "into the rooms" of NA and AA and took the 12 Step program seriously. I had attended many types of spiritual events in an effort to find my answers. Even when I was younger, I somehow knew instinctively that my problem was spiritual.

Once, when my mother and father took my brother and me to Atlanta, we had attended the church Martin Luther King went to regularly. We were among the few white people there. Everyone had on gloriously big, ornate hats. Not only did I want one of those hats, I also wanted what I thought these folks had. They sang with such fervor and joy. So when the preacher asked if anyone wanted to be "saved," even though somewhere deep inside of me I did not think I was worth saving, I rushed up to the pulpit, almost tripping on my feet, and stood on tenterhooks, hoping this would be my salvation. It didn't happen like that. I was disappointed and just felt conspicuous. I felt every bit the hypocrite, even though I did not quite have a grasp of what that meant.

"Regretting the past or chasing the future is a useless exercise," I recalled one of the women at a 12 Step meeting saying.

"Stay in the moment; it will help you remain grounded," the voice of another one of my spiritual advisors sounded in my head. It had resurfaced against my will.

"Shit, I think I enjoy obsessively rehashing my past and feeling miserable just out of habit!" I said to no one in particular. Not even Satchmo seemed interested in my ranting.

I was a social worker who worked with abused and neglected children and their families. You'd think I had some sort of insight into the concept of Post-Traumatic Stress Disorder. But the old adage "Physician heal thyself" seemed to slide off my shoulders like an unwanted shroud.

***

When Travis died, I had taken some time off work and found I was glad that I had. Maija was flexible. She knew instinctively that I was on the verge of coming unraveled. She also knew the burnout rate in our field of work was high. I'd been there for three years. It was the first job I took after graduate school.

"Rachel, we are worried about you. Please take some time off. You haven't taken a vacation in a while, and you still have plenty of PTO," she said, her eyes unflinching. It felt more like a directive than a choice.

And more often than not, I listened to Maija. She had a way with me like a cowboy with a wild bronco.

It was Maija who introduced me to the rooms of my first 12 Step program. She had friends "in the rooms."

Maija had also inspired me to get my GED and go to college and graduate school after both my parents were killed that day in a freak airplane crash on their flight to Moscow.

And it was Maija, after serving as a GAL for fifteen years, who accepted a position as the director of a non-profit group working with abused children and families who offered me my first job after I finished graduate school. She knew some people questioned her decision to hire me, but she did it anyway, which made me love her that much more.

"Who would be more perfect working with these kids and their families but someone who has lived through some of the same crap?" she asked me, always believing more in me than I did in myself.

But, as in a lot of mother-daughter relationships, I did not tell her everything. Either by acts of omission or boldface lies, I always tried to invent a more favorable picture of my life. I could never bear the thought of disappointing her.

* * *

When I was not even 17, I was diagnosed with severe clinical depression and given electro-convulsive therapy (ECT, or "shock treatment," as known in some circles). It was assumed, since depression ran rampant in my family and I had not responded well to anything else, that this would work. Electrodes were placed on my scalp while I was under a general anesthetic, and then a finely controlled electric current was applied. It was supposed to induce a mild seizure, which was supposedly the fastest way to relieve my symptoms, especially because I was suicidal. I had already tried to kill myself twice. Once I had cut my arm with a pair of dull scissors so deep it required fifteen stitches. I still have some numbness in my fingers because I cut a tendon. Prior to my parents' deaths, I remember attending "family day" with them. It was a three-day psycho-educational workshop to include family therapy—supposedly to educate and promote healing and to address the complexities of my co-occurring psychiatric disorder—depression and addiction. I had to attend a separate track from my parents, and then we came together to process what we learned.

"I realize that Rachel has to take ownership of her disease and the obstacles she is facing and will continue to face," the male therapist, Dr. Boone, said to my parents. "But I want to talk about how you can help her with this. During the course of this workshop, both of you have negated many of the underlying premises of this disease and have expressed some unrealistic expectations about what Rachel needs to do. I perked up automatically. I felt I was being validated and defended, and I smiled slightly while my eyes filled with tears.

Instinctively, I tried to shut my tears down and turn off the faucet.

"That is the biggest crock of nonsense I have heard," my mother said, sucker-punching me in my heart. "We don't expect any more of Rachel than she can produce. As parents, we just want her to live up to the potential we know she has. She refuses to adhere to any reasonable rules or restrictions; she lies, she manipulates . . . maybe part of that can be attributed to this "disease" you've preached to us about . . . but I'm not sure we could have done much of anything differently to show her we care."

"I understand how difficult it must be to watch someone you love drown and not accept the life-preserver you throw out to her . . . but she has her own life jacket, and with support, insight, dependable resources and commitment, she may learn how to float. You have to provide clear, consistent boundaries coupled with a positive outlook, which, admittedly, is hard. When the overall mood of your family home is decidedly downbeat and any positive behavior is overlooked, Rachel may unknowingly decide the best way to get attention or even brighten the mood is to create a crisis. It tends to reinforce the substance-use disorder, which she may be also engaging in as a way of self-medicating," he said looking my mother directly in the eyes.

"I understand what you are trying to say but am not sure I necessarily agree—" my mother started out, shoulders squared off as if facing an opponent in the ring.

"Rachel, does any of this make sense?" the therapist interrupted, which I sensed infuriated my mother. My father didn't say anything. In fact, he was looking out the window.

"I have never felt supported by my mother," I said bluntly, with a twinge of regret.

"That is absurd! Nick, have we not done everything these so-called professionals have asked of us? I love you, Rachel. Am I a perfect parent? I should say not. But I have done everything I have known how to do—" She stopped suddenly, glared at my father who did not respond, and then at me.

"Never?" Dr. Boone asked me without engaging my mother.

"I guess that isn't true *entirely*. She just doesn't seem to notice when I do something right, but whenever I screw up, she jumps on it like a dog on a bone. She thinks I am stupid, and so I act stupid!" I defended my inaccurate belief system.

"Rachel, I don't think you are stupid," my mother said. "Far from it. I just don't think you apply yourself and are ruining any future chances you might have. We just want the best for you as does any parent." I thought I heard her voice quiver.

"That is right, Rachel," my father said as if on cue, "we don't want to watch you self-destruct and break under such little pressure. Life is filled with trials and tribulations that are meant to be overcome not succumbed to."

In the end, we did have a better understanding of one another but were not able to implement it very well. Time was sliced thin because they were killed. And I was not only left with my unsettled feelings toward them, but a grief and sense of guilt because I had not made amends. I also hated God for taking them away; I just wasn't insightful enough, due to my developmental years, to know that I hated Him.

So, the slew of mental health professionals decided I needed shock therapy due to the diagnosis of clinical depression they had assigned me. I now suspect my symptoms were due to penetrating grief coupled with depression, and because of my continued substance use, I was not sophisticated enough to process that grief. I vaguely remember this period in my life. I can recall certain sensations: the smell of sour alcohol; the taste of a hard, wooden tongue depressor; bright florescent lights making eerie buzzing sounds; and a milieu of people's faces. After the shock treatments, I had continued mild seizures and the doctors prescribed medication to subdue them. I tended to carry around a pocketful of resentment like a hard stone plucked off the side of a mountain. All that the shock treatments seemed to do for me was make me forget certain situations that had aggravated my depression, but not the hollow ache of the depression itself. Depression still causes my mind and body to collapse on itself without warning even with my Welbutrin. Our 12 Step promises assure us that at some point in our recovery we will "not regret the past nor wish to shut the door on it." But as a recipient of shock therapy, I didn't and still don't remember the whole story, so, sometimes I get lost in the first chapter. Shock Treatments steal memories.

But somehow Maija's calm determination to love me back to wellness began to have a positive impact on my internal belief system. And when I started to experience some small successes, I believed I might succeed. But even with my forward progress, there always seemed to be periods in which I slipped back into my old ways. Believing I deserved to succeed was quite different from believing I might succeed.

As I sat with the grief of Travis, my mind tumbled farther back through time. I remembered some of the consequences of my repeated falls from grace. Actually, I would jump from grace. I had been "in the game" on and off throughout undergraduate school. Still, I managed to keep my passing grades and was not divorced yet. There was a little bar and grill close to the campus, and I found my way there more often than not. It wasn't much to look at—a hole in the wall with a screened-in porch jutting out from the side. The patrons consisted mostly of bikers, a few smatterings of students who partied like I did and a hodgepodge of other wayward souls.

One evening I had been at it hard and was driving around with a couple other folks I had picked up along the way, all looking for mischief, all talking a mile a minute with the music blasting. I turned the corner way too fast, tried to over-correct and the car went air borne. We ended upside down with the front end of the vehicle resting dangerously against a telephone pole. Somewhere along the way, I had picked up a little person whose nickname was Midget, although we all knew that was not politically correct. He scuttled off into the night after I wrecked, as his pockets were loaded down with illegal substances. When the police arrived, I chose to undo my seat belt just as one of them shined his flashlight into my car. I was in a daze and was unaware the car was upside down so I went crashing into the floorboard. I ended up in the drunk tank, moaning and crying about being an "alcoholic." This did not seem to sway anything in my favor. My driver's license was suspended, and I ended up having to do some time in the local jail. Since I knew my exams would be at the time I would be incarcerated, I asked one professor if he would bring it to me in jail. When he arrived, they allowed me to go retrieve it and take it in my cell. It was for my Deviant Psychology class! I sheepishly shuffled up front in an ochre colored, button-up smock dress with one of the buttons missing, the kind someone might wear to clean offices; an old army blanket with a hole in it wrapped around my shoulders; and plastic slip-on sandals. It was demoralizing and ironic, but now it just makes me laugh.

*   *   *

It was a miracle that my marriage to Jon lasted the seven years it did! Some may talk about the "seven-year itch," but my marriage was more like an infestation of fleas the entire seven years we were together. He enabled me to continue indulging my cross addictions—alcohol, cocaine and whatever substance was available. He bailed me out and occasionally even got high with me because I became very much the seductress when I was high. I had periods of sobriety and clean time, but because he was neither alcoholic nor addict, he could drink and sometimes smoked pot. He kept his boxed wine in the refrigerator. I seethed with resentment that he could drink with impunity and I couldn't. We began to fight over absurd things, and in the last year we were together, these fights had escalated into physical altercations. I was just as physically assaultive as he was, although since he was bigger and stronger, he had the advantage. Once, we got into a heated discussion about vocabulary over what some call a "wash cloth." At first, I referred to it as a "wash rag" and he corrected me with what I perceived as a tone of superiority, indicating it was a "wash cloth," not a "wash rag."

"A rag is something you use to dust with, Rachel. A wash cloth is what you bathe with," he admonished.

"Oh, who gives a crap? Only *you* would be concerned about that!" I shot back.

We hurled insults and punches at one another until we were both bruised and broken. Another time, we fought over cornbread. He thought I had cooked it too long. I had made the entire meal from scratch and was in no mood for *constructive* criticism. He ended up breaking one of my prize possessions, a jewelry box my father had given me that was his mother's. In retaliation, I nailed the cornbread, which really had been cooked too long, to the wall and pulled some of the crust off to portray a smiley face. It was worth the black eye he delivered. After these incidents, he always wanted sex and was rather demanding about it. I became convinced that the only thing he was interested in me for *was* sex. And I would hurtle all sorts of verbal grenades at him because of this belief. I could not stand him even looking at me, let alone touching me. Since both of us married at a young age, we were not equipped to deal effectively with any issues of significance. We were just too immature, and I was too broken.

One Friday night, after coming home late from work, I found my husband, Jon, glued to the computer. I stood behind him as he masturbated while watching porn. I had caught him indulging this obsession on a couple of occasions and each time he promised he would not do it again. He lied. I became enraged. I threw things and shouted obscenities that I didn't even know I knew.

"You fucking pervert! Flanging your dong while you devalue women . . . you were so self-absorbed you didn't even notice me standing behind you. What kind of creep are you?" I implored, still hoping he would scoop me into his arms and tell me it would be all right.

I cried. I pulled out pieces of my hair. I slithered down into the corner of the room with pieces of my hair sticking out of my fist like turkey feathers.

My performance was worse than any acting Paris Hilton, socialite and reality television host, has done. And Jon walked out quickly with not so much as a word.

He came back later and retrieved his belongings. I had been pacing the floor, hoping I had not chased him away. He glared at me as he stepped through the front door.

I started to apologize, "I'm so sorry—"

"I really don't give a shit," he interrupted. "I am tired of feeling nasty and perverted. I look at porn because you won't let me look at you. You can't even take your clothes off around me. I'm done." And with me following close behind, he gathered up a few belongings, muttered under his breath, "You are one crazy bitch," and left. Soon after this encounter, he stopped by the house when I wasn't home and got the rest of his stuff and some stuff that wasn't his and filed for divorce.

It was Maija who came to my rescue. Even though we'd managed to glue me back together with outside help, the glue was no longer holding. Little by little my façade seemed to be crumbling. I was still ridiculously devoted to my work, had an empathy for my clients that ran so deep it was almost embedded in my bone marrow. I could think out of the box, sometimes producing a miracle. But I was having a hard time keeping up appearances and breathing underneath my mask.

I had a relapse or two that neither Maija nor my work knew anything about after my marriage dissolved. My sponsor in my 12 Step program questioned if I was still in a relapse—whether I was actually picking up a drink or drug or not—since I was not being honest about it!

At the last staff meeting at work that I attended right after the divorce, I kept interjecting my viewpoint about a case involving a sexually exploited teenage girl until my voice was one decimal short of a scream. I then got up abruptly, pushed myself away from the table and said, "I don't need this shit!" and left. Luckily it was Friday afternoon. I disappeared for two days, and went to a nearby town, drank copious amounts of liquor, slept with some nameless man and returned feeling worse than I did when I left. Surprisingly the incident was overlooked and I still had my job. I'm sure I was the center of office gossip, at least for a short time.

△

*If you do what you've always done,
you will get what you've always got.*
12 step program wisdom

As I sat in my house, tripping over Travis and the black hole of sorrow over his death, I looked down at my feet. I had on one striped Halloween sock in shades of orange and black and another plain black sock turned inside out. I shook my head free of regrets and laughed so hard that my nose started to run and I started coughing uncontrollably. I sat down on the faded hardwood of the deck, which Travis never got around to staining. Satchmo, for the second time that day, started to lick my face and nudge me, hoping for a biscuit.

"God, I wish I had a cigarette," I said, knowing I quit smoking almost two months ago.

Funny, I had been smoking since I was ten years old, and the only reason I gave up cigarettes was I had my teeth whitened, and I didn't want to ruin my smile. This time, my obsessive vanity had produced a rather favorable result. The fact that I had Hep C and my liver could not expunge the bad toxins deposited from cigarettes was never reason enough to quit even though my doctor had advised that I should.

Men seemed to like my smile. I knew I looked good with my thick auburn hair, green eyes and dimples even if I secretly hated the ground I walked on. Looking good was a way I exercised some control over a life that seemed so out of control. I could always work out, watch my figure, dress just a little provocatively and flirt. But somehow, it ended just like my drug and alcohol use, in a perverted ride to hell. It opened me up to repeated victimization in the long run and would never completely take away all my painful memories.

Travis seemed to take great pride in my looks, I remembered. "You're the best looking thing in this part of the country," he would simper.

And even though my best judgment knew it to be a lousy pick-up line, my heart still melted.

"How long have you been clean?" he asked, his blue eyes searing my heart the first day we met.

"I relapsed during and after my marriage imploded . . . It was a hard crawl back . . . I have been clean almost three months," I responded with mild trepidation, expecting him to either want to save me or run screaming into the night.

"I have three months tomorrow! Wanna be there when I pick up my chip?" he inquired with pleading in his eyes.

After the meeting, we went to Cracker Barrel to eat. I was still smoking then, and he chain-smoked Camel cigarettes. Cracker Barrel had great vegetable soup, good prices and a smoking section. It seemed like a no-brainer to us. We stayed for almost three hours, talking about our past, our present and our future—in jargon only recovering alcoholics and addicts would use. Travis used touch to emphasize a point, and it would shoot little bolts of electricity throughout my skin.

Travis picked up his three-month chip the next evening. I didn't want him to know how smitten I was with him, so I sat with the women like the old-timers in recovery told me I should do even though I knew it was all a pretense. I never fully followed directions in anything I did. I would manipulate and lie, and I felt smart enough to convince those around me that my reasons were legitimate and made perfectly good sense. I did not focus on my recovery. I did focus on Travis and imagined what it would be like to kiss his full lips.

Travis sauntered up to me afterward, and I gave him the obligatory hug for his efforts. I thought I was sincere, but I still had no full understanding of what my real motives were, and frankly, I did not care.

"You feel good," he breathed softly into my ear. He could have had his way with me then, if he had known.

We were almost conjoined twins from that day forward. I felt we were both philosophically profound and that I had found my spiritual equivalent. In hindsight, it seemed absurd that I had convinced myself we were philosophically profound, as neither of our brains were fully developed after the years of neglect caused by our addiction. In reality, it was uncertain whether we would have been able to tell the difference between a sweat bee and a butterfly. We discussed prose from Kahlil Gibran's *The Prophet*, debated C.S. Lewis' *The Screw Tape Letters* and conferred on Carlos Castaneda's *Journey to Ixtlan*. We declared ourselves transplants from another era; we were convinced we were sixties' generation hippies at heart. We analyzed our own behavior, made comparisons to the program literature and gasped at each other's innate wisdom. But mostly, we fondled, stroked and mauled each other's bodies every chance we could.

After about a month in our relationship, we were coming out of a meeting when an old, white, rusted-out Ford drove up in the parking lot. I recognized the driver from my "party days." Brian was tall, skinny and covered in tattoos. His hair was dirty. With a rubber band, he had pulled it back tightly on his skull into a ponytail.

"Travis, man, I've been looking for you," he barked out the window.

Travis had been distracted the entire meeting and had been texting on his phone. "Well, you found me, eh?" Travis interjected while climbing into the beat up car. Absentmindedly, he said over his shoulder, "Babe, I've got some business to attend to . . . I'll catch you on the flip side." And off they drove.

I obsessed about where he was going half the night. I worried about him all the next night and hardly slept. And by the third night, I was frantic. I called everyone I could think of in the 12 Step rooms that knew him and then started calling my "stash" of people I knew outside of the rooms. Work helped to distract me when I was there, but there was plenty of time to indulge my obsession after work.

My attendance at meetings started to drop. I quit calling my sponsor. When she called me, I did not return her call. Eventually I stopped going to meetings all together.

"One drink couldn't hurt . . . it's been a long time," my one voice whispered in my head. In the recent past, I automatically dismissed it once I recognized its intentions. But I seemed unwilling to do anything I had been taught to use to tame it. I certainly had no intention of going to a meeting. And I was convinced prayer would be a ridiculous exercise in humility because once again I was convinced that no Creator could love me. I was simply unlovable.

After two weeks of not having heard anything from Travis, I stopped at the ABC on my way home from work. It wasn't even on the way. It was as if my car was on cruise control. My head seemed void of any thought at all. I just went in, grabbed the cheapest whiskey I could find and made my purchase.

When I got home, I closed the shades, unplugged the phone, fed Satchmo and poured myself a drink in an old canning jar I used as a glass. I didn't adhere to any two-finger rule. Half a glass of whiskey and a splash of Diet Coke and I was good to go. I downed the entire thing in one gulp. I grimaced. I never liked the taste. I didn't care. A couple of drinks later, I decided that I should try and find Travis.

"Satchmo, you wanna go for a ride?" My words jumped out like a ghost in a spook house. Satchmo, didn't seem to care if I was drunk or sober; he loved me unconditionally.

I carried my bottle out to the car and stashed it under the seat. By this time, I didn't care if I had a chaser or a glass. I went back inside and got Satchmo, put his leash on and put him in the car.

"Hey, we need to cruise by Becca's house and see if she has anything for the head." Satchmo cocked his head to the side as if he knew what I was talking about. I fumbled around and found Becca's number still listed in my contacts. I called.

"Yup?" Becca answered in a way-too-loud voice.

"Hey there, girl!" I hiccupped and then laughed also way-too-loud.

"Rachel? Oh, my God, I wondered what happened to you! I missed you, woman!"

Becca was an old running buddy. She was a switch-hitter and liked both women and men. Hell, she just plain liked sex, or so she said. I suspected she was broken like me. Becca sold drugs to supplement her own habit and her minimum wage job she held part-time at the local convenience store, THE FAST-STOP. A lot of her customers made arrangements to meet her someplace after work. The store was located right next to a strip club. Becca always took pride in "not taking a dump at my place of legitimate business!" Sometimes Becca would strip, but only when she needed the extra cash. She had extraordinary grace and had always fantasized about being a professional dancer.

The old-timers in the meetings stressed the importance of "changing old playmates and playthings," but I guess I had not been willing to "go to any length" for my recovery. Even though I hadn't called any of them in a long time, I did keep several "playmates'" numbers in my cell phone. Just in case...

It was like I had never been in a treatment center or the rooms. I drove up her graveled driveway, singing to Aretha Franklin. I loved old blues and had my iPod filled with BB King, Stevie Ray Vaughn and Otis Redding. The car hit a rut in the road. I cursed and tried to avoid scraping the bottom of my car. I stepped on the gas deciding that was the best course of action. The car bumped and seemed to take flight, occasionally spitting gravel and dust as it did.

"Sing with me, Satchmo... R E S P E C T tell me what that means to me?" I bellowed as I came to a screeching halt at Becca's front door.

I noticed, as I clamored out of the car and let Satchmo out, that there was a truck parked next to Becca's Ford Escort. I reached under the seat and pulled out my bottle, unscrewed the top and took a drink.

"Hmmm, I wonder who is here..." I hoped whoever it was, he or she had a cigarette.

As I stepped into the small clapboard house, I was bombarded with the familiar odor of marijuana combined with a mustier odor of patchouli. Becca was busy rolling a joint while Susan Tedeschi played on a CD. Becca had similar taste in music and loved all things vintage. She was an old soul. *And if I'm an addict, she's an addict,* I thought.

Looking up while simultaneously twisting the end of the joint she finished rolling, she smiled, her eyes glazed.

"Hey, wild thing, what's going on?"

Satchmo scooted past me, not knowing a stranger, and practically jumped up in her lap. She laughed noisily and began to talk to him in a childish tone.

"Why do humans always talk baby talk to animals?" I asked, not really expecting a reply. I kind of stumble-danced my way toward her. "Baby cakes, you is looking good!" I looked her up and down appreciatively.

Becca had highlights in her brown hair that looked almost natural, golden brown eyes, and a full bosom. Even though she only had a high school education, she had street smarts and was funny to the bone! Becca could have gone to college. She had been offered a scholarship but just never found her way there. I always flirted with her, but we both knew my heart wasn't in it.

"Pull up a seat and sit a spell . . . do you know Dan-the-man and Larry his sidekick?" she asked right before taking a big toke off the joint she had just rolled and passing it to Dan.

Dan was a huge block of a man with a goatee. He took a hit and passed it to Larry, who was sitting on the big, worn sectional next to him. I noticed Dan's eyes scanning me up and down. He nodded, and then said in a very Southern drawl, "Hey, darling, where you been all my life?"

"Damn dude . . . ain't you got anything better than that?" Becca scolded. "She's way out of your league anyways! You are so dog-stupid when you are high! It's almost embarrassing! Satchmo has more sense than you!" She laughed and rubbed Satchmo behind the ears. "Fix yourself a drink, sweetie . . . we are getting ready to do a bump if you want to try it before you buy it! I know you don't really like weed, so I won't even ask if you want a toke," she declared as if trying to get Congress to pass a bill.

I sashayed my way to her kitchen. Becca didn't have much money, but for someone from what my Sociology Professor coined a "deviant subculture" she had good taste. She read voraciously. I could see well-worn paperback copies of Wally Lamb and Barbara Kingsolver and tattered Herman Hesse novels lining the shelves of her bookcases. She had meticulously placed pieces of local, hand-glazed pottery intermixed with her book collection along with pieces of driftwood and various-sized glass terrariums.

When I got to her kitchen, I poured a shot of tequila into a tumbler with a splash of tap water. I never thought once that mixing it with the whiskey I had already sucked down might not be such a great idea.

Becca was pulling out a metal box from under her chair when I returned moments later. In the box she had some baggies already divided into "eight balls." There was a small, square mirror, a delicate silver coke spoon, some scales and some straws. She pulled out a bigger bag filled about a third full of coke and opened it. She deftly got out what she wanted, divided it up into equal lines on the mirror and triumphantly motioned for me to do a line.

After a little while into the thing, we were jabbering away with each of us talking over the other. Getting high made me feel connected to people I might normally just like a little. While high, it was as though I had served on the front lines with them in a major battle.

Dan kept leaning into me as if what I said was of profound interest, while occasionally cooing, "You are gorgeous . . ."

I didn't really pay him any extra attention, but I loved flattery and being an object of desire. Suddenly, as if my thoughts had an on-off switch and someone accidentally bumped into mine and turned it on, I blurted out, "So, do you know Travis Manson?"

Dan's eyes seemed to roll around in his head for a minute. "Yeah, I know the dude. Not well, but we've partied some together. Why?"

"Well . . . ah . . . he and I were an item and he sort of disappeared. I was just wondering if anyone knew something I didn't," I inquired with hope gathering at the corners of my eyes.

"Baby, you sure can do better than him!" Dan salivated, closing in for the kill. "He's strung out bad and serving as Brian Henry's gopher I hear."

Dan passed the joint to me as he blew smoke out the corner of his mouth.

"So where is Brian hanging these days?" I asked after I took a gulp of my drink. "Is Travis staying with him or is he holed up somewhere else?"

"Slow down, gorgeous! Brian lives in his father's old farm near the Madison County line. His father passed away a couple of years ago and left him the house with fourteen acres. It's off Leicester Highway. You know the place?"

"Yeah. I think I scored there a time or two in the past. Is Travis staying with him?"

"I think so. Come on, baby. Wanna ride down that way and have a look see? I sure wouldn't mind giving you ride. I'll drop Larry off on the way, and we could take the scenic route to Brian's place. I got plenty of blow for the ride and we could stop and get a bottle to wet our whistle."

As if reading my cues, Becca interrupted, "She ain't going anywhere with you! I'd be surprised if you can keep that truck of yours between the lines and your dick in your pants!"

I smiled nonchalantly and said as if I had at least considered it, "Naw, Dan, I know how to get there. I think I'll sit and visit with Becca for a while before I go anywhere. Thanks anyway." It was always amazing to me how I suddenly straightened up when I wanted something. And I always wanted to be wanted, so it was with reluctance that I listened to Becca.

Out of nowhere, Larry shouted, "Hey, dude, we were supposed to pick up a part for my bike, remember? We need to get going."

"Oh yeah, excuse me, ladies. I almost forgot," Dan apologized, belched as demurely as a big guy could, got up and headed for the door. Larry was on his heels.

"Good riddance!" Becca snarled as they departed in their truck, windows rolled down and Eminem rapping into the dust.

"Rachel, I'll take you down there. You don't look like you need to drive," she said, tucking a lock of my hair behind my ear. "You do look good, though," she purred into my ear.

Even though a fog was definitely forming between my ears, I instinctively knew I should just go home and nurse what would probably be a killer hangover. But, like I was on automatic pilot, my feet started moving and words kind of popped out of my mouth like kernels of corn in a microwave. "Let's go, honey bunny! Bring some of that blow with you. Here's some cash to cover it," I said as I stuffed a couple of twenties in the palm of her hand.

Satchmo started running around me in circles, nub tail wagging, making his whole backside rock side to side. Satchmo loved me regardless of what state of mind I was in, and it always brought me great comfort. God I loved my dog! Compared to dogs, people always seemed to have a hidden agenda and expected you to know what that agenda was.

We piled into Becca's Escort with Satchmo sticking his snout in between the two front seats, expecting the special place between his ears to be scratched. I obligingly scratched him there. Even though Satchmo loved me unconditionally, my heart still felt guilty that I was taking him along on this misadventure. He was like my child. But I chose to ignore my feelings and lit up a joint. Becca cranked up the engine, whipped her car around, and we headed out the driveway.

"Rachel, are you sure you want to do this? Girl, I'm not liking the effect Travis has on you. I mean, he took off and left you high and dry ... fuck him!"

For just a moment, I reflected on past relationships and how I always seemed to be in one, but how they never seemed to complete me like I thought they would. Initially, I would be filled with excitement and a sense of belonging. They always seemed to end with what felt like a total disconnect. But I still would obsessively try to preserve them even though they had long since emptied of anything worth preserving. I never saw things as they truly were until they fell apart.

"Oh, I dunno what I am doing, but I am doing it with determination!" I stated.

Becca shook her head, Satchmo shook his body, and I shrugged involuntarily.

I stared vacantly out the window at the landscape. North Carolina was really beautiful country. Luckily we'd overcome the previous years of drought and had two years of substantial rainfall. Everything was either emerald or deep forest green. The mountains hovered in the distance with hues of purple and the North Carolina-blue sky sat on top of them like a mother gazing softly at her child in its crib.

Normally, when I was clean and sober, Satchmo and I would take full advantage of a day like this and go hiking. I had always meditated in the woods. Nature inspired a spiritual awakening. I never did fully grasp the concept of quieting the mind and sitting in a lotus position as a form of meditation. I still remembered arguing with Travis over the novel, *Eat, Pray, Love* that insisted meditating was easy once one got the knack of it or at least that is what I read into it. Later on, someone explained that meditating was detaching from your thoughts, not stopping them. This was a concept I did not relate to. I just could not, or refused to quiet my mind or detach from my thoughts unless I was surrounded by nature's palette.

Instantaneously I was jolted back to reality. Everything seemed surreal. Sadness crept over me like scales on a lizard's back. For the second time in a short period, I shrugged as if I were trying to rid myself of fleas.

I searched Becca's cooler for a beer, popped the top and downed the entire thing, wiping my mouth with the back of my hand. Suddenly, the car crashed into something, made a loud thumping sound and lurched to the side of the road. Becca was frantically trying to get control of the wheel as the car swerved, kicking up dust and gravel. It finally screeched to a sudden stop at an odd angle on the side of the road.

"What the hell?" Becca implored.

We both scrambled out of the car to see a rather large rabbit decapitated in the middle of the road.

It made me think of the cartoon Bugs Bunny and Elmer Fudd's quest to make Hasenpfeffer. I started to snicker. Then I started to cry.

"Should we let someone know we killed it?" I said, my words colliding with one another.

"Geezers, Rachel, it ain't a puppy!" Becca said, looking at me incredulously. "I guess we could dig a hole and bury it." Becca was like a Boy Scout and always seemed prepared. She got a portable shovel out of the back of her trunk, and we took terms digging. We, for some reason, emptied the cooler and put the rabbit in it and stuffed it in the hole, barely covering it back up with dirt. I poured a little beer over the mound, and turned up the can and drank the rest in a sort of toast to the rabbit. I then sang a broken version of "White Rabbit." Becca shook her head at me.

We arrived at Brian's "farm" three warm beers, one joint and a line of coke later, if one could call it a farm. Clunker cars, old appliances and discarded junk littered the yard like pebbles on a shore. The house itself was in total disrepair. Paint was peeling, the windowpanes looked like they had never been washed since installation, and some of the boards on the porch were missing.

"Oh, my . . . Brian must have started selling meth again," Becca said to no one in particular.

Satchmo didn't seem to care and started pacing frantically in the back seat, just waiting for someone to open the door so he could go exploring. A pit bull in a pen by the side of the house started to bark.

Brian, skinnier than I had last seen him, covered in zits and just plain mean-looking came out on the porch, pointing a gun.

Becca yelled out quickly in a panicky voice, which was uncharacteristic for her, "Geez, Brian, I texted you and let you know we were coming. Quit being a psycho and put down the gun!"

"Well, you never can tell. Get your ass inside, bitch, and bring that hot mess with you!" Brian said as he watched me sort of fall out of the car with Satchmo at my heels.

"I told you to never call me bitch, you dick!" Becca snarled back. Becca emulated bravado at the oddest times.

"I was just kidding," Brian replied and then laughed hysterically. His pupils were dilated, and he seemed to be scanning the horizon for unseen enemies.

We all went inside. A wood stove sat in the middle of the room, with the coals from a recent fire burning in it even though it was a warm, summer day. Dirty mismatched curtains covered the windows. It was dark. The odor in the room was a combination of urine, pot, booze, smelly feet . . . and something else I couldn't quite put my finger on.

"Who is your decorator?" Becca asked.

I laughed and hiccupped at the same time. I felt uncomfortable but chose to ignore the feeling. I looked at Satchmo. He was trembling. I instinctively offered Brian a line of coke as a sort of peace offering. He obliged with robotic mannerisms.

"Shit, sweetie . . . this is just child's play. I've got the real stuff!" He went into the recesses of the house and came back with a lock box.

"You can pay cash now or pay later, if you get my meaning," he said as he stared at my crotch, looked up and drooled. He then pulled out a glass pipe that looked like it had been used repeatedly and did his thing. He dragged on it hard and heavy as his eyes rolled back in his head.

For some reason, I had a moment of clarity—or grace—and mumbled, "No thanks . . . uh, I was just wondering . . . is Travis still staying with you?"

Brian stared at me, and I could feel a hole burning its way through my head. His eyes glazed over and turned solid black. "Fuck him! Who gives a shit about him? We are right here, right now!" Then he turned and growled at Satchmo. "Get that mother-fucking dog out of my house!"

Satchmo startled and backed up against me, shaking like a magnitude 7 earthquake. I looked at Becca imploringly as if to say, "Turn and run!"

Becca piped up, "Hey, man, that's unnecessary. I've fronted stuff to you many a time . . . you don't need to rip us a new asshole. We are out of here!" She got up and motioned me to leave. Satchmo was already at the door before I could get to my feet.

"Get the fuck out, you stupid bitches, before I throw you out," Brian spewed.

Neither of us needed another warning. We both trot-ran to the car, stuffed Satchmo in the back seat and left. Darkness was starting to hang in the trees as we sped away.

The air hung with anxiety. I found one of the warm beers rolling around on the floor in the back seat and popped it open. Foam exploded from the opening and saturated my pants.

"Well, least now you can't tell I peed in my pants!" I said with not even a hint of humor.

"We both gotta quit this life . . . it's gonna get us killed!" Becca shared with tears streaming down her face. "Sometimes, just sometimes, I can almost visualize me turning my life around. I don't want to do this, really I don't. I just don't know how to be anything else."

I looked at her like I was seeing her for the first time. She really was beautiful and worth saving. It felt good to be thinking of someone besides Travis or myself.

"Becca, there is always hope. I forget that. You suppose you could just take me home? I really don't feel so good," I said as my head started to swim and my gut started to buckle.

In the early morning hours, as I lay on my couch, trying to recall the events of the day with a mouth as dry as Satchmo's kibbles and bits, I vowed I would pull it together and "cease and desist " as my father used to say. A towel covered with vomit and blood lay on the floor next to the couch. A sour smell wafted in the air. Satchmo was curled up at my feet snoring lightly.

The last couple of times I had gone on a bender, I had been more than sick to my stomach. I wondered, for a brief moment of concern, if my liver was acting out the torment I put it through. My gastroenterologist had emphasized that drinking and drugging was not good for someone with Hep C and an ulcer. Out of habit or denial or both, I dismissed that train of thought like a choir director would someone who was tone deaf.

I could not remember if Becca had taken me home right away or not. I called out her name, and it seemed to bounce off the walls. Satchmo lifted his head and his backside started wiggling back and forth.

I got up and took Satchmo for a walk so he could do his business, and I realized I still had no clue where Travis was, if he was coming back, or if he was dead or alive. I started imagining all the possibilities, and not one of them was making me feel so good. Then I just plopped down on the ground and started crying uncontrollably. Satchmo tried to sit on my lap with his leash all tangled up around me.

* * *

Almost one month later, I got the phone call about Travis being dead. I still had not gone back to any meetings and had been drinking alone at the house. I had an array of opiates to "help me sleep" and amphetamines to "wake me up." I worked copious hours. I felt like crap most days, and hell the others.

Detective Ross was efficient and thorough but not outwardly compassionate. He grilled me day and night for days and then just stopped with no explanation. The autopsy report indicated

Travis had been murdered. He had suffered blunt force trauma to the head. The toxicology report indicated all sorts of illegal substances had been gurgling to catch their breath in his veins. At first, I called obsessively to find out if there was any new news on the case, but then just quit. My addiction seemed to have a hold around my neck. So, on this particular morning, as I stared transfixed on a daily meditation book, *As Bill Sees It*, lying on my table, it seemed apropos that Debbie, my sponsor, would appear at my door.

Debbie always said, "I will never work harder than you do," but there she was with Maija and two other women from the program.

I stared at them in disbelief, feeling a little self-conscious over my appearance, but not enough to contain my curiosity

"What are you doing here?" I demanded, not offering to let them in. I was standing in the door frame with my hair tangled so badly a crow could have built a nest in there and no one would have been the wiser. I kept chewing on my tongue as if that might keep me from dissolving into the floor like the Wicked Witch of the West. Their stares awakened some desire to be civil, so finally I invited them inside.

"This is a 12 Step call, Rachel," my sponsor said without blinking.

"What makes you think I need anyone calling on me?" I demanded, knowing full well what the answer was.

"Oh, Rachel. Sit down, sweetie. All you have to do is listen with an open heart. It's not too late to start over. We want to help. Besides, if you could see yourself, you would probably agree you could use some help." Debbie smiled slightly with compassion filling her eyes and then scanned the living room. Dirty clothes, crumpled tissues, plates—with dried moldy food on them—empty beer cans and liquor bottles littered the living room. Debbie knew this was out of character for me. I kept my home clean and was obsessive about it. I had always enjoyed decorating, and my home was filled with an eclectic mix of antiques, contemporary handmade furniture, original art and craft pieces and a beautiful rug I inherited from my father's trip to China. I was an artist myself, and some of the artwork displayed was my own. A gallery owner I knew had encouraged me to exhibit my work, but I was convinced no one would come and was afraid to take a risk.

"Whatever you need to say, just say it. Don't try and pretty it up. I'm not sure I could stand it if you were too nice," I said, feeling dejected.

After about an hour of listening to Debbie and the other women share their "experience, strength and hope," I agreed to go into treatment. I even begged to go into treatment. I was filled with such remorse and self-loathing one could almost touch it. My lip quivered as I softly cried and Maija gathered me into her arms. I had felt so damn cold and couldn't seem to warm myself; this was the first time I had felt warm in weeks.

Prior to coming to see me, Debbie had already made the arrangements for me to go to a treatment center, so I couldn't come up with any excuses. It had a medical detox as part of its program. She had already spoken with my employer, and Maija was going to watch Satchmo and house sit.

***

I spent a longer-than-average stint in detox because my withdrawal was hard. However, treatment seemed to breeze by. I knew the drill, but had the "gift of desperation" and was willing to apply what I had learned in my life. I still struggled with shame and "regrets" but accepted it might be awhile before I could let those go. I needed to reconnect with my spiritual side. I knew that I could not do it by myself. I needed help from something bigger than me, but could not connect with that if I was in the throes of my addiction. I remember someone in the program stressing that if HOPE, being one of the principles behind our 12 Steps, was an acronym, the "P" would stand for "power"—the power of my creator, the power within and the power to change. I can't remember what the "E" stood for, but I think it meant "evolution" after I embraced that power. I was hopeful.

During family weekend, my brother, Thomas, came to see me. Maija brought him. I had not really spoken with him in a good year, and before that it had only been out of perceived obligatory family duty. I had resented him for so long that I had not even taken the time to get to really find out who he was. I did not think he loved me. So, when he came to see me at the rehab center, I was shocked.

Thomas was a criminal defense attorney. In the past, I always had felt he was interrogating me. Today, he was different. He hugged me and surprised me by saying, "God, I thought we'd lost you, and I realized how much I need you in my life." We talked for about an hour, as he searched my face for answers to why we had lost one another. The last time I had seen Thomas, I had been drunker than drunk. I had gone to Atlanta essentially to "play" someplace other than my "backyard." I wasn't there to visit with my brother. To be truthful, I was using his place to crash. I remember I was trying to pretend I wasn't doing what we both knew I was. I tripped into his house in the wee hours of the morning. I was in his kitchen rifling around trying to find something to eat.

Thomas came in and started asking questions. I replied in a less than sober voice, "Fuck you . . . you always think I am up to no good! You think you are holier than thou!" I used this line way too often. It occurred to me I was spreading peanut butter on a piece of bread with a huge butcher knife. I tried to make it look like I had intended to do so when I fumbled the knife and somehow it ended up stuck in his wood floor between my feet. I abruptly left everything where it was and stumbled to bed. The next morning Thomas interjected some healthy boundaries and informed me I was not to come visit if I couldn't stay clean and sober. I told him to go fuck himself and did not go back.

Thomas was a big bear of a man although he had always been gentle and forgiving, traits I wanted. I was glad he was able to forgive our last meeting and had come to see me in treatment. He told me what he had learned in the family education workshop he attended that morning at the rehabilitation center. I shared that even though I wanted to recover, I was not sure I would or could but was trying to keep focused on "today." It was a good visit.

* * *

When I got released, I did not follow all the aftercare recommendations because I was convinced I needed to return to work and get my caseload back in shape. I did attend meetings regularly but was still trying to run my life my way. I had accepted that drugs and booze had made my life unmanageable but did not think my life was unmanageable in and of itself. It was no wonder I was struggling. I wasn't being honest or telling on my disease. So, when my boss volunteered me to take some time off from work, I think she was hoping I would head my addiction off at the pass before it got its hands on my throat again. But I instinctively knew I was walking a thin line at work and that seemed to hold my attention more than most things.

I picked myself off the deck, after sitting there in the sun rehashing the past, and walked back into the house. Before I could think about it, I forced myself to call my sponsor and asked her to meet with me.

"I am scared . . . I have not used, but I am having a hard time convincing myself that I care if I live or die," I declared, one word falling on the other. "Can we get together and do some work on the steps? I need to redefine my relationship with a Higher Power."

"Sure, kiddo. I was praying you would come around," Debbie acknowledged.

* * *

A couple of months into my recommitment to recovery, I was just starting to believe that my life could change and maybe, just maybe, the God of my understanding loved me. Then, as fate always seems to do, it challenged me.

It was a Friday. I had the day off as I had already worked fifty hours that week and had some flextime. I was puttering around the house with Satchmo on my heels when I got a call from Detective Ross informing me that they had acquired enough evidence to charge Brian with murdering Travis.

"Rachel, we are charging Brian with second degree murder," Detective Ross stated. "He confessed. It wasn't a well-thought-out plan, just drug-induced stupidity and rage. It really is a sad commentary on human existence," he elaborated with a tone of exasperation in his voice.

"Oh, well thank you," I responded. ". . . I guess . . . I'm not sure what I can say to that." I thought I had come to terms with Travis and had done some good step work to help me deal with my feelings. These feelings of loss, shame and guilt had been a constant, unnamed hurt that sat heavy in the pit of my stomach for a long time. I had sifted this one hurt into another bigger bowl with other hurts I had accumulated over time. It was hard to distinguish one from the other.

According to Detective Ross, there was no real reason why Travis was murdered other than he and Brian had been smoking both crack and meth and their higher self seemed to have been obliterated. Brian not only confessed, but also showed Detective Ross what he had killed Travis with. He had smashed in his skull with the poker he used to stoke the fire in his wood stove. Brian had not tried to hide or destroy the poker; he was using it the day Becca and I went out to see him. The odd smell that Becca and I smelled in Brian's ramshackle house that day was Travis's decaying ring finger. It had the sterling silver and onyx ring I had given him on it. Brian coveted his ring and could not get it off, so he chopped off his finger. Detective Ross insinuated that I might be subpoenaed for court. After I hung up, I sat in a daze for what seemed like a long time, just rubbing Satchmo behind the ears while he "sat watch" at my feet. He instinctively knew how much I needed him. I called Maija first and in a monotone voice related the story. She indicated she was coming over and would not take no for an answer. I then called my sponsor, Debbie, who also insisted on coming over.

"It will work out the way it is supposed to work out," Maija pronounced. Maija sat on my bent willow rocker and gently rocked back and forth.

"You are not responsible for the outcome," Debbie added. Debbie was sitting surrounded by pillows and in an Indian-style posture with her legs crossed and tucked under her thighs on my oversized club chair. Damn, she is flexible, I thought with a seed of irritation planting itself in my brain. Quickly, I hacked it down. I knew better than to water it, or it would grow out of proportion, and then I would be seething with resentment for no real reason other than envy. Instead, I forced myself to try and listen and be grateful I had people who cared and loved me even if I seemed unlovable to myself. After a while, my shoulders started to relax and were no longer up above my chin.

I went to work that following Monday and was going to meetings regularly, but I was having trouble sharing any real part of myself. Debbie tried to pull the real me out during our individual meetings. We read the fourth addition of *Alcoholics Anonymous* together, highlighting paragraphs of interest. She even had me try my hand at journaling, but I was as dried up as a scab about to fall off.

I poured myself into my job and my clients. I organized, created, advocated, facilitated and linked my clients to resources. I was almost mesmerized by their pain and searching and had a hard time separating myself from my work

One young girl in particular, Samantha, had attached herself to my heart like Spanish moss on a tree in the Deep South. She had white blond hair, fair skin and sky blue eyes, which if you looked closely enough, had the startled look of a young fawn who hears shots fired in the woods. She lived with her mother, who shacked up with one man after another, drank more than her share of liquor and smoked crack. Samantha had been sexually abused by at least one of the men and physically abused by her mother for "getting in the way." No one was the wiser until her teacher caught her masturbating at ten years old while sitting at her desk in her classroom. She was removed from her mother's residence and did her tour of foster homes, but because of "incorrigible" behavior, she was placed in a group home. On one occasion, I was called because she disappeared from school. They had found her on the roof scrunched up into a ball, staring into space, rocking back and forth. She loved to rollerblade, but in fits of rage would take the blades and run them up and down on the dry wall and then hide under the bed and not come out. I encouraged her group home staff to have her earn the privilege of using her rollerblades when she learned to channel her anger better. I volunteered to take her rollerblading after she had made some good progress. I even began to indulge the idea of becoming a foster parent myself so I could take her into my home and "make her whole."

It was a good thing that my boss took the initiative and invited me to take some time off before I actually started the process of becoming a certified foster parent. I did not have what she would have needed me to give to her on a full-time basis. Unfortunately, the system later gave her back to her mother, and I heard through the grapevine that she had become pregnant at the age of 15. I carried some of these sad stories around with me like a sack of cement. It was helpful that there were a couple of success stories in my repertoire to water down that cement.

"Get into action!" my inner voice chastised. I decided to weed my rock garden and clean up the yard Travis had littered with his cigarette butts. Travis and I had built a small landscape pond. I loved gardening and was good at it. I had made some mosaic stepping-stones leading up to the pond and rock garden. As I got on all fours, Satchmo stretched out on the moss under the huge oak tree nearby. I had planted some impatiens, which were spreading nicely. Moss gathered here and there on the surface of the rocks like it had come out to play, and other annuals poked their heads in between like chaperones. I had also added some shade-loving perennials including astilbes that produced wonderful, feather-like flowers. A garden always made me think of my grandmother. I recalled that she had been an avid gardener. I could visualize her gathering up her gardening tools, gloves and the over-sized straw hat that she placed on her head. Grandmother had long, wispy, gray hair she braided and wrapped around her head. Each night she took it down and brushed it, and each morning she put her hair back in the braids and meticulously wrapped them around her head. It was always the same routine, and that comforted me. She worked in her yard for hours. When I visited, I trotted behind her as fast as my little, chubby legs covered in Band-Aids carried me. She let me be her "assistant" as she tended to her garden. But that never lasted long. I could never stay in one place. I would be up chasing squirrels, convinced that if I ever caught one, they would delight in being my pet. I sometimes hunted for rocks to add to the collection I kept in the pipe tobacco tin my father gave me. Or I would sit in the crook of my favorite tree and make up stories about my life. She never seemed to mind and, in fact, always chastised my mother for being "too hard" on me whenever she tried to rein me in. I idolized my grandmother who, unfortunately, wasn't in my life long, and it caused another sting on my heart that I wasn't able to dissipate at my young age. I still remembered she had a wrought iron sign that read:

> KISS OF THE SUN FOR PARDON, SONG OF THE BIRDS FOR MIRTH,
> YOU'RE CLOSER TO GOD'S HEART IN A GARDEN, THAN ANY PLACE ON EARTH.

As I worked on my own garden, I watched two squirrels chasing each other around the base of a tree. Birds sang in the higher branches. Calm inched its way up my body, instead of the usual disconnected nerve endings making it hard to be still. Tears welled in my eyes—not tears of sorrow, but tears of release. I prayed in silence, "Thank you for all the blessings you've given me, which I am not so sure I deserve." I was grateful for just being alive and knew that I could have died several times and had not seemed to care one way or the other. Now

I cared. I wanted to live life fully. That in and of itself was amazing. I was given yet another chance. I knew my prayer was heard. I could finally let go, if only for the moment, and I would remember how good it felt to let go from then on. I had always held on tightly to any hurt, real or imagined. I would not allow myself to feel it for fear it would strangle me and all I would be left with is my inability to breathe. All I ever could identify with was the struggle itself or being a victim. So, in that moment, the act of letting go was so liberating that I felt as if I could fly—I was weightless.

That evening, after a good salad and some fresh broiled salmon with just the right seasoning, I almost bounced into my 12 Step home group. I had picked this group to be my home group because of its convenient location and proximity to my house, the years of clean time most of its members had and the emphasis on the spiritual underpinnings of recovery. And my sponsor had told me I needed to commit to a home group and get entrenched in service work.

I came early to make coffee and set up the chairs. Debbie arrived shortly after me and said out loud, "Well, lookie here . . . lately you have been coming in late and leaving early . . . it's good to see you get here early." She gave me a big hug, and I hugged her back just as furiously. She pulled me away from her with her hands on my shoulders, looked me in the eyes and said, beaming, "Oh, there's my girl!"

"Thank you for being patient and believing in me," I said with a little crack in my voice.

I shared where I had been, what happened and where I was now. I cried. I laughed at myself. And I was surrounded by hope, unconditional love and acceptance. It felt good to be back.

△

You are not alone.
12 step program wisdom

TIME MOVED FORWARD. I had ups and downs, as is life, but my program seemed to evolve, and I started to change. It had been more than a year since Travis died and a year since I last used. Debbie always emphasized that I should do recovery "one day at a time," and that is what I did, recovery being a program of action. I did it even when my brain screamed at me that life was "unfair" and I was "not worth the effort," and I wanted—and even sometimes felt like I needed—life to be other than what it was or people acting other than I thought they should. Slowly, I no longer believed myself to be the center of the universe, although at times self would boomerang back and hit me full force between the eyes. I now was willing to do what I knew would help me deal with the insanity of my thinking. I had accepted I had a brain disease but that my brain was resilient, and I could carve out new ways to think and believe—like a whittler would on a piece of soft wood. And

Debbie was always be there in the background to admonish, explain and cajole me to see things from another perspective. My 12 step literature supported Debbie's, message and I listened with a fervor that I had not claimed in the past. I wanted what Debbie and others at meetings who were in recovery had. I was so exhausted chasing myself over hot coals. So Debbie asked me to tell my story after I picked up my one-year chip.

I had long since returned to work, but was working at a more reasonable pace. I found out that a niece of a colleague of mine was struggling with active addiction. Joanne, her aunt, was someone I had admired without telling her so. She seemed earnest and authentic and had an easy laugh. She always did her work with little or no complaint. Our clients seemed to like her. In a non-offensive way, she always encouraged me not to call the people we worked with "clients" because that might be considered a derogatory term.

"How would you feel if I related to you as my client if I was your therapist?" she asked, eyes unflinching.

"I dunno. I don't think it would affect me one way or the other if you were a good therapist. If you weren't, I probably would think you were belittling me," I replied without giving it much additional thought, except to say, "What would *you* call them?"

"By their first names," she said gently.

Joanne heard me offhandedly mention to another colleague I was scheduled to tell my story, and she asked if she could come. It was an open meeting, so family and friends were welcome to attend.

Her brother, Mike, came with her. He was a substance abuse counselor at a treatment center across town. It was their sister's daughter, Julia, who was in a boxing match with her disease. They brought her with them. Her mother, their sister, Mike's twin, had died in a car accident two years before. Her father had died of a "freak" heart attack a couple of years prior to that after playing racquetball. He apparently had quite the cocaine habit that no one liked to talk about. Mike was Julia's legal guardian and Joanne was his pinch-hitter. I found it beyond noble that her brother pushed to become Julia's guardian. He and both his sisters were quite close, and Julia, according to Joanne, thought Mike "walked on water."

At the end of the meeting, my colleague Joanne introduced me to her brother and her niece. Julia was 16 going on 40. She had dimples, curly brown hair down to her shoulders and a heart-shaped face. She was absolutely adorable and moved my heart the first time I looked into her eyes.

He squeezed my hand after hearing me give my talk. "I related to you completely, and your journey really inspired me," he said with a face as earnest as the sky is blue. "Hopefully Julia got something out of it as well." His eyes were blue-gray and filled with honest regard. His hair was starting to get some silver at the temples. I figured he must be in his late thirties or early forties. He was solidly built and had a smile that was infectious. Mike was an attractive man, seemingly on both the inside and outside. And ironically enough, he was a substance abuse counselor with ten years of sobriety. I found it interesting that I was attracted to him because I had always liked taller men and he wasn't but three to four inches taller than me.

I introduced Julia to some younger people in the program who instantly wrapped themselves around her like foam insulation behind dry wall. Mike knew some other members at the meeting and drifted off to speak with them and shake their hands. Joanne and I stood by as Julia was surrounded by a group of young women who were giving her their phone numbers. I scanned the room and saw Mike talking with another man somewhat younger than he. He seemed to be leaning into him, intent on hearing what he had to say when he spoke. He really knew how to be present in the moment. Just when the man turned to leave, he looked up and our eyes caught one another. I blushed as he smiled at me.

Joanne needed to talk, so I listened. She shared openly how, as a family member of someone with addiction, she wanted to either fix the problem or pretend it didn't exist. Story upon story about Julia's parents, her brother and Julia fell out like rancid buttermilk from a cracked pitcher. I remembered having overheard Maija venting to one of her best woman friends about some of *my* escapades. One of them must have been particularly painful for Maija I realized right at that moment while listening to Joanne.

I had been in college. I was loaded up on booze, coke and then dropped some acid. I was hallucinating and depressed at the same time. I remember trying to cross the street. There was a crosswalk. I had to press a button to stop traffic to go to the other side. At that moment, I was convinced I could experience death and not die . . . a delusion for sure. However, at the same time, I wanted nothing more than to die. There was a security guard somewhere in this memory. According to him, I tried to pull his gun, which was secured by a holster with a snap. His version, which I don't completely recall, was that I was screaming about dying as I tried to pull out his gun. Of course, I was handcuffed and ended up being involuntarily committed. Maija, my guardian, was called in the middle of the night by hospital emergency room staff. I cannot imagine the hurt and frustration she must have felt. So as I listened to Joanne, my heart stung, knowing the pain we cause others when we are in the pits of this self-centered disease.

A couple of weeks later, after conversing with Joanne at the meeting, I was with some friends hiking with our dogs when I ran into Mike on the trail at Bent Creek. He was with Julia. Satchmo ran right up to them and around them in circles with his hind end waging back and forth and his nub tail trying its best to keep up.

"Well, aren't you a friendly thing!" Mike interjected.

Julia bent down. "Mind if I pet him?" Satchmo rubbed against Julia's leg and then sat down almost right between them. She laughed easily and starting cooing at him and rubbing the special place between his ears. He looked at her affectionately.

I introduced Mike to my friends who agreed to forge ahead without me. They had already received an earful about Mike, and so they knew it was their cue to leave when Mike asked if we wanted to join Julia and him for lunch.

We went to what Mike called "good country cooking." On the acreage behind the restaurant, it had a vegetable garden, some strategically placed, raised flower gardens flanked by rock walls; and a greenhouse. They rented cabins out. A stream wound through the property. There was a quaint, little, hand-forged covered bridge crossing the stream that led to a pasture where the restaurant proprietors kept their horses. They had used gnarly old branches from the mountain laurel that grew on the property as pickets. Homemade apple butter was served with the best slap-your-mother-in-her-face buttermilk biscuits I'd ever eaten. I decided right then and there to forgo my commitment to a healthy reduced-starch, low-fat diet. There were fresh veggies, so I convinced myself that eating squash casserole, country beans and meatloaf was a good choice "just for today."

Mike and Julia had an easy relationship. I could tell they adored one another. Julia had been going to meetings every day and I could already see the change taking place. She smiled more genuinely, her skin was clearer, and she expressed her feelings out loud. We seemed to talk on a deeper level than other people who had only known each other for that short a period of time. That was the thing about recovering people: they gained a new family that had its foundation based in honesty and intimacy.

"So, I didn't know you liked to hike, Rachel," Mike said. "I love all things outdoors. I have a two-person canoe and would love to take you down the French Broad next weekend. I could pack a daypack with stuff to eat and drink. What do you say?"

Julia looked up at Mike with a mischievous smile and said, "Yeah, what do you say . . . of course it would just be the two of you 'cause I have other things to do and don't want to always be seen with a bunch of old fogies!"

I laughed along with Mike. "Sure. That would be fun," I said nonchalantly as my stomach did a flip and my heart started racing.

I had to admit, I missed the company of men. I had followed directions this time around, and just hung out with my women friends for over a year. Still, Mike was not the usual caliber of man I associated with. And my heart knew this was a good thing.

Mike called me Saturday morning to get directions to my house. He arrived on time, which was a definite point in his favor. He brought me a frappe, which endeared him to me even more. Drive-By Truckers was blaring out the window as he drove up. That made my heart skip a beat. I love Drive-By Truckers and had seen them live on two occasions.

My mind fell back on itself as I recalled the last time I had gone to this concert, I think Jason Isabell was playing with them, but I could not be sure because I was as saturated as a Kleenex used by someone with a summer cold. Almost by myself, I had drunk half of my friend's beer keg at the "party before the party," had a few shots of Tequila—lime optional—and a nose full of coke. I think I may have also smoked some crack, but could not be certain.

I had dressed in my concert attire, which meant lots of beads, boots, braids, suede and even a cane with a hole bored into it through which I had looped a piece of rawhide to hang a small cow bell on. I went with one set of folks and ended up with some others. In my excitement, I whooped and hollered, took another swig from some concoction that was being passed around, swung my cane around my head, almost decapitating several folks near-by, and promptly passed out.

I woke up in an isolation room so-to-speak.

"Where's the party?" I yelped right as my eyes opened. My voice sounded muffled like a trombone with a mute.

"You passed out and took a few people down with you when you did," an official-looking character I could not quite see snarled. "We can't decide whether to arrest you or send you to the hospital. You definitely need to stay here for observation."

Immediately I tried to get up. I was unsuccessful and sort of slithered around on the thing I was lying on. Of course, I have no clue to this day whether it was a bed, a gurney or the floor.

"I'm fine. Just let me go on home if you aren't going to let me back in to see the Truckers," I woofed, trying to look mean.

"Young lady," the officer growled back at me like the principal at my school used to talk to me, "you are not allowed back in there, AND, as I said before, we are trying to decide whether or not to arrest you. If this gentleman will sign for you, I would rather be spared the hassle and send you on home if he assures me he will take you to the hospital if you go out again."

"I can sign for myself!" I spat out while I wormed and twisted myself from a prone position. A toddler learning how to walk would have been more graceful. Of course he ignored me while he spoke to a young man whose long thick hair was in a braid. He had a Drive by Truckers t-shirt on. He had pretty eyes and winked at me in a secretive way. I realized I had no clue who he was.

He was beyond polite, saying, "Of course, I will take care of her and make sure she gets home. I don't want anything to happen to her. I apologize for all the inconvenience and scare. Thank you for your care."

I agreed for him to sign me out, pretending that we were the finest of friends. He signed some sort of form clarifying that the organizers of this event would not be sued should I die. Both of us laughed about it in a demented way afterward. I think he even urinated in a potted plant container outside the arena where the concert was held. We ended up partying all night at some hotel close-by, having sex in strange positions and listening to Drive-By Truckers. My nose was running constantly by the end of the evening, and I blew it hard into his tube socks that lay on the floor. I'm sure he got a surprise when he put them back on. I snuck out before he woke up. I never did get his name. My body was sore for days from the aerobic sex workout. I don't know if we used protection or not. I do know I was elated when I started my period.

* * *

I hastily shelved this earlier memory of the Drive-By Truckers and focused on Mike, giving him my best impression of an angelic smile.

I learned later on in the day that Mike played both the mandolin and guitar. I played an old Kimball upright piano and my mother's acoustic guitar that I had restrung. Neither of us would go on the road anytime soon, but both of us thoroughly loved music. Then, there were the times Mike would just randomly start whistling, which I found comforting and sexy all at the same time.

We talked about recovery as he drove, but with an honesty I had never before shared. I was never testing him like I had done with so many other men in relationships in the past—regurgitating my past to push them away. I felt comfortable and at ease. Mike was easy-going, funny and humble. There was no pretense about him.

"I'm not in a habit of asking girls out in the program and never anyone who has less than a year," Mike said as he looked me in the eyes. "My sponsor always warned me that hitting on girls with less than a year was not thirteen stepping, but *no* stepping. Still, something about you made my heart skip a beat and my mouth overruled my head. After I found out you picked up your one year chip, I couldn't stop obsessing about you. I don't know if that was my disease or your bewitching powers."

I just smiled. The consensus in 12 Step programs is that a newcomer (someone with less than a year) needed to concentrate on her recovery and was not clear enough to make healthy decisions, especially when it came to relationships with the opposite sex. That being said, any one of the opposite sex who "hit on her" was thought not to be working a good program and was taking advantage of her vulnerability.

"There was a time early in recovery when my mouth always overruled both my head and my heart," Mike continued. "I was convinced I was an accident waiting to happen and that there was no cure for what ailed me. So I isolated myself to avoid hurting either myself or anyone else."

I did not interrupt to spit pieces of me at Mike. I listened earnestly.

"My dad was an alcoholic. The mean kind. My mother was an angel. I used to drink with my dad 'cause that was the only time he seemed to want to spend time with me. He was a crude, violent man. I don't know how my mother put up with him. He treated her like shit. I hated the way he treated her. My sisters and I both did. But that was no reason for me to become a repeat offender. Of course, then one thing led to another and I started smoking crack. I didn't understand this thing called addiction. I thought I was just morally twisted like my dad and tried my best to act like I didn't give a damn . . . so I hurt those I loved. You know where the Big Book, *Alcoholics Anonymous*, talks about not regretting the past nor wishing to shut the door on it? I don't shut the door on it, but I sure do regret the hurt I caused those I loved. I'm so thankful they had big enough hearts to forgive me."

"Yeah, for a long time I didn't think anyone cared anything about me, so I didn't think I was hurting anyone but myself," I related. "I was just that self-absorbed. Of course, I have regrets, only I'm just now figuring out what those are."

I could feel the tears starting their dance in the pit of my stomach, but I threw a blanket on them. Instead, I reached over and brushed his hand with mine and our eyes locked for just a minute before he turned them toward the road.

"I always thought I had a handle on this thing or that I was just too damaged to care," I continued almost without taking a breath. "It has taken me a long time to accept that it is a disease. In fact, I was always finding ways to dispute it. When they talked about the progression of this disease, I found loop holes in my own story. I always drank and drugged to excess from the get-go.

Maija, dear Maija, sat me down and had me watch this film *Pleasure Unwoven*, which is by a doctor who also suffers from this malady. It convinced me I did have a disease and was not a moral degenerate. And then I started making my own necessary connections with my story. Even though I always drank and drugged to excess from the get-go, I was able to consume larger and larger quantities and the consequences seemed to become more and more severe."

"Of course, then we still have to have the willingness to do something about it," Mike interjected. "Who is Maija?"

"She is my earth mother," I responded. "She took the time to love and believe in me when it felt like no one else would. I have put her through hell and yet, she still comes back for more," I then proceeded to explain who exactly she was and what she meant to me.

"I would love to meet her," Mike said.

* * *

When we set out on the river, we both were mesmerized by the noise our paddles made when we put them in the water and the sound of nature all around us. It was more than peaceful—ethereal. To eat lunch, we paddled the canoe over to a secluded spot by the river that was consumed by emerald green moss. Of course, Ms. Grace, trying to show how tough and adept she was at handling a canoe, got out to pull it up the bank, slipped and sat down in the water. We both started laughing at once. I laughed so hard that I started snorting and crying at the same time, which made Mike laugh that much harder. He pulled me up out of the water with such force, I practically fell on him. That is when he kissed me. It seemed so natural. I fell into it with such enthusiasm, it took him by surprise. And there we stood making out, with slime and river muck stuck to my backside.

"Mmm . . . you taste good," Mike whispered. We gazed longingly at each other for a minute.

"Speaking of tasting good," I said, breaking the moment before I lost my resolve to play a little hard to get, "what's for lunch?"

I could tell by the bulge in Mike's jeans he wasn't as interested in lunch as I was convinced I should be.

"Uh . . . all sorts of cheeses, homemade bread, homemade pickles, carrot and raisin salad, and red velvet cake," he replied almost sputtering.

Mike opened up his day-pack, unraveled a blanket and spread it on the moss. Carefully, he took out little Tupperware containers and laid them on the blanket. I was impressed. He even had napkins and a towel for me to dry off with.

"I have fallen in the water a time or two myself and learned to be prepared," he said with a lopsided grin.

Conversation between us was as easy as if we had grown up together. We even burst into song when we were talking about our favorite musicians. Our voices seemed to complement one another and both of us smiled as if the corners of our mouths were playing tag with our ears when we finished singing.

"You have an amazing voice," Mike said.

"As do you . . . ," I mumbled as we found each other's lips again. Since it was getting late we pulled apart and headed back.

When he took me home, he kissed me longingly as we stood on my porch. I made a split-second decision that I should not invite him in. He was a gentleman of course and declared that I would be hearing from him again soon.

After walking and feeding Satchmo, I piled into my bed and found the book I had been reading. I couldn't concentrate. I kept thinking about Mike, the day and how well he kissed. Suddenly, my cell phone started its usual jingle.

"Hello?" I said.

"I told you that you would be hearing from me again soon," Mike said.

We talked for almost an hour, said goodnight, and I fell into a sweet slumber with Satchmo's head on my leg.

Mike called me frequently, but not every night, which I thought showed good boundaries. Travis and I had pursued each other relentlessly and would not go a day without seeing or contacting one another. It had been the same way with my ex-husband. It was probably about time to exercise some discretion.

Mike and I found time in our busy schedules to go hiking, bowling, exploring art galleries and dining at restaurants. Once we went on a zip line adventure. We played our guitars and sang with friends and went to meetings. Still, other than some heavy making out, we had not made love. Of course, that didn't mean we didn't want to.

We were just waiting for that right time. We were falling in love.

One Friday evening, Mike was at my house as I prepared him one of my favorite pasta dishes. He tossed a salad filled with radishes, cucumbers and cherry tomatoes from my small garden. Satchmo sat almost on our feet and begged for a treat when I shooed him out of the kitchen. I gave him a rawhide bone to chew on.

"Baby, let's go to the coast for a weekend. I know a really nice bed and breakfast in Charleston. I want to take you deep-sea fishing. What do you think?"

"When?" My green eyes blinked back at him. I hoped he couldn't read my mind because I was already thinking lustful thoughts.

I was also scared. I still had trouble identifying my feelings and had a tendency to deny them. Instead of accepting them, I put my feelings on the witness stand and judge their validity. Even though I had read a lot of those *Psychology Today* articles that suggested feelings are not facts but need to be felt, I somehow put myself in a box that even Houdini himself could not get out of.

My sexuality had become almost a separate identity—as if I was reading about it in a romance novel found discarded in a cheap motel. I did not feel comfortable in my body and felt I dissociated whenever I had sex. That did not mean I did not know all the tricks and maneuvers or that I appeared frigid. It just meant I thought sex was a means to an end. I thought it was a form of power and control.

I recollected, with some restrained rage—like a boxer in the ring, who had just been punched repeatedly in the face and finally managed to back his opponent against the ropes, checks himself from breaking any rules called by a referee—a memory about a male psychiatrist I had been assigned to in order to address my issues of sexual and drug abuse.

It was during my college years. I had attended a rather obscure college initially—Pfieffer College in Misenheimer, North Carolina—before transferring to UNC-Asheville. It had a highway that ran down the middle of the campus, separating the male dorms from the female dorms.

The incident when Maija had rescued me from the hospital emergency room and assisted me in getting the care I needed, occurred after I had taken some blotter acid (LSD) and drunk copious amounts of alcohol. I had been traipsing around in the male dorm against the rules when some of the male students yelled, "The dorm manager is coming! You need to leave!"

I was already in the beginnings of what was called a "bad trip" because the LSD was supposedly laced with strychnine, which I learned later was a myth propagated by drug users themselves or anti-drug crusaders. When I started to cross the street between the campuses, another student pressed the button, which changed the light from green to red so students could cross. I believed I could stop traffic and that started a whole chain of illogical thinking. I was convinced I could fend off death. In an effort to prove my point, I fixed on the security guard that just happened to be at the crosswalk.

I tried to pull his gun, but it was fastened down by a snap and would not pull free.

"I have powers beyond all powers. I am finally free within this power," I fulminated. "Nothing can stop me as I transform this life."

Naturally, he arrested me, as I was in the throes of the psychotropic effects of the acid, and I kept chanting these absurd rantings about being immortal. He had to wrestle me to the ground to get the handcuffs on my wrists. The officer thought I was trying to kill him, I suppose. I tried to reason with him, explaining my superhuman abilities and my desire to test it out on myself.

"I am filled with light and am not trying to hurt anyone. I just wanted you to witness the miracle."

These words didn't seem to dissuade anyone from committing me. It was Maija who actually signed me in—with a gentleness akin to a butterfly lighting on a flower. But I greeted that gentleness with caustic words.

The psychiatrist who was assigned to my case had an apartment close to the college campus. He allowed students at the college to frequent his small dwelling and would party with them. He invited me with the pretense that "if I needed to talk" more than the scheduled sessions near that hospital once I had been discharged, I would always be welcome there.

"I've found that there are times, other than traditional office hours, a soul just needs to shake itself free. I am available at any time, night or day," he said, looking like a dog licking its genitals might look. I took him up on his offer. He supplied me with pot and occasionally some cocaine. And he always had beer. I provided him with sex even though I was married to Jon at the time, a fact I conveniently forgot. He didn't seem to be bothered with any ethical considerations. "Doctor P," as I called him, was in his forties, had bleached blond wispy hair that was long in the back and balding in front. His legs seemed shorter than average, and I imagined he didn't have much luck with women he encountered in his world. So he took advantage of opportunities presented. He was just another zit in a face full of acne. Men were not to be trusted but could be manipulated. I held that as my truth. Although at 18, I am not sure how sophisticated or insightful I was, I was unaware of my intentions and the intricacies of my heart and mind. I operated on instinct and just wanted to feel good and not sit naked in pain.

But Mike had stirred a feeling in me that had long-since been put away. It had been buried under layers of hard earth. Mike seemed to have unearthed my need to connect, to feel, to release . . . to trust.

"I was thinking Labor Day Weekend," Mike replied softly. I could hear his breathing and wondered if he could sense my anxiety, want, fear, need and desire all mixed in a turbulence together.

"That would be lovely. You make the arrangements," I said in a surprisingly even tone.

Even though it was a couple of weeks away, and we still planned to hang out in-between, I knew I would not give myself to him until then.

I went to my office that Thursday because I had asked for Friday off, and poured myself into my work. But I seemed to float a few inches off the ground the whole day and was not as present for my clients as I usually was.

During an individual session, one of our adolescent girls who had been a client of mine for a couple of years, called me out on it. "Hey! Wake up! You are always harping on us to be fucking mindful of what the other person is saying, and you look like you got ripped last night or laid one," she said with a sarcastic snicker.

Her words startled me. I was amazed at how perceptive she was. "You are right," I said. "Sometimes I need to follow my own advice. I'm not perfect and I apologize. I'm glad you feel comfortable enough to call me out on it. What great progress you've made to be able to ask for what you need!" I quickly added, trying to get the focus back on her. I cleared my head of Mike and turned my attention to her and the art-therapy homework I had assigned her the week before. It turned out to be a good session even if it did start out a little off-centered.

After work, I went to my favorite spa and treated myself to the "manager's special," which consisted of a pedicure, a manicure, a facial and getting my hair trimmed.

"You have gorgeous skin and hair," Angie, the hair stylist, cooed. Another woman sitting next to me, having her hair done, added, "I wish I had your hair and skin . . . I bet you drive the men wild!" An abstract thought appeared out of nowhere. I wondered if somehow I had consumed so much alcohol it had somehow preserved my skin like cucumbers in vinegar . . . I had been pickled. I started giggling. Angie looked at me inquisitively with one artfully red-dyed eyebrow rising slightly.

Still, I somehow felt more vulnerable and uncertain about my looks than usual. Even though on occasions my bravado had me thinking I was "hot," I now felt like a teenage girl with a huge fever blister on prom night.

I went to Belk's at the mall, hoping to find sexy, but demure lingerie for "our" weekend. I selected a silk, azure-colored, floor-length gown with spaghetti straps and a plunging neckline. It had darker indigo lace and reminded me of something Betty Grable might have worn. The clerk indicated I looked stunning as I stared into the mirror in the dressing room hallway. I bought the gown, some lacy panties with matching bra and a black bikini with a subtle embossed print.

Mike picked me up early the following morning. He looked tan and relaxed, confessed he had "hardly slept much at all" and smiled. He loaded my bag into his back seat, and off we drove.

During the ride down to Charleston, Mike periodically became agitated with other people's driving and shouted obscenities, then apologized, laughed at himself and turned up the music. This made him seem even more endearing because there was comfort in knowing he was not perfect.

We settled into a comfortable silence after gabbing non-stop for about an hour. I looked out the window as the landscape changed. I briefly thought of Satchmo. I hoped my friend who I paid to dog sit would remember to give him the stuffed, squeaky toy that I bought because we were leaving him behind.

We drove up to a beautiful bed and breakfast inn flanked by stone pillars, a pig iron fence and trees weighed down with Spanish moss. I vaguely remembered a tour my mother had taken me on when I was a child somewhere in the Deep South where the tour guide gave a discourse about how the pig iron was made. Molten cast iron would run directly from the base of a blast furnace into a sand trough that fed a number of smaller side troughs; this arrangement resembled a sow suckling a litter of piglets, and cast iron produced in this way then came to be called pig iron.

As I stared at the inn, I sighed out loud. "Oh my . . . this is absolutely stunning."

"Yes it is. It looks even better than it did on the Internet. Aren't I nice?" he inquired with a sweet smile.

When Mike took me into his arms that night after a day of sightseeing and eating our way through Charleston, I succumbed totally and completely. It was amazing. I thought of the woman who wove grass baskets at the market. She did not want us to take her picture for fear it would capture her soul. I was always afraid that if I gave myself completely to a man, he would somehow steal my soul and I would lose myself forever. It never occurred to me that I had been lost, and letting go helped restore me to myself. Tears streamed down my face. Mike traced the tears down my cheeks with his finger. He did not interrupt my tears. He gazed at me softly, and with tears in his eyes whispered, "I love you."

The next day we went deep-sea fishing. Mike had chartered a ship dubbed "Staci Mae." I had never been deep-sea fishing. Of course I took some Dramamine before the cruise. Initially I felt a little green around the edges, but luckily overcame it. A few other passengers did nothing but puke, so I was grateful. Mike had a tendency to want to instruct me throughout the day on the intricacies of catching the "big ones." That was a little annoying. I learn better by trial and error and tend to prickle when someone is telling me what to do. But when I listened to him, I actually fared better. He wasn't doing it to be annoying; he just wanted me to catch some fish. We didn't catch the biggest fish, but we caught enough grouper, snapper and amberjack to make any seasoned fisherman or woman proud. We took a whole bunch of pictures of us with our catch and then of the fish themselves. I wasn't sure why Mike insisted on taking so many pictures of fish, but I thoroughly enjoyed watching him enjoying himself.

When we returned home with our share of fish that Mike had filleted, packed in freezer bags and put on ice in a cooler, I knew that we had begun a new chapter in our lives.

Mike began to spend most weekends and evenings at my house. He had stained the deck that Travis neglected, and together we had cleaned up the yard and completed some other needed repairs around the house. He even put in a double-sink vanity in one of my bathrooms.

Almost two months after our trip to Charleston, we were interrupted by the shrill ring of Mike's cell phone that was charging on the night table next to our bed.

"Whattt . . .?" he answered sleepily. He sat up in bed. I stirred awake, knowing instinctively something was wrong.

"I'll be there as quick as I can," he said.

"Julia over-dosed on heroin and is in intensive care," he said in a quivering voice.

We gathered up our clothes strewn by the bed, got dressed and drove to the hospital. Neither of us said a word. I reached for Mike's hand, and we held hands the entire drive there.

Joanne, Mike's sister, met us in the emergency room. Her eyes were red-rimmed and wet with tears. Her face looked pinched. We hugged tightly. She started sobbing.

One of the things I loved about Mike was his tendency to let people feel their feelings without interruption. He just hugged her and rubbed her back until she was done.

"Can we see her?" he implored.

"They are in there with her . . . it doesn't look good." Joanne sat down with us.

We waited helplessly and it seemed that time had gone on an unannounced vacation. Mike went up to the nurse's desk periodically to try and get some information and came back each time like a deflated balloon.

"They are still working on her."

Suddenly, a man came out of the closed metal door with a surgical mask hanging around his neck. He spoke to the nurse, who said something back to him and then looked directly at us and sighed loudly.

We all stood up at once as he approached.

"I am sorry to have to tell you . . . we did everything we could . . . but we couldn't save her," he said in a dejected voice.

"What are you saying, man?" Mike bellowed. Mike's face turned red then a ghostly white as tears escaped from his eyes and flowed down his face.

I was detached from the entire scene and just observed. I was numb. I was afraid if I felt anything, I would not be able to give anything to these two people who had become my family and whom I loved more than anything in the world.

"Fuck, fuck, fuck . . ." Mike repeated over and over. Joanne crashed into him and started wailing inconsolably.

The doctor stood there looking uncomfortable. I could see pain sitting on his face, and I knew he was a good human being to the core. He had become a doctor for all the right reasons. In one instant, I had a deep respect for him.

"Thank you for all you tried to do," I mumbled as Mike and Joanne struggled to regain their composure.

"Yeah, thank you. When can we see her?" Mike asked.

My heart ached for him. Talk about feeling powerless. There was nothing I could say or do to make the hurt go away. I followed Mike and Joanne blindly. I wanted them to have their time with Julia and offered to wait, but they both seemed to want me to come with them.

Julia lay on a steel gurney in a harshly lit room filled with machines beeping and buzzing. The nurse turned around and closed the curtains. She spoke in a kind but professional voice. "Take all the time you need."

Julia's curls seemed to have lost their spring and were matted against her head. Her heart-shaped face looked the same but not the same. I felt my throat constricting. Mike stroked her face and pushed a wayward curl off her forehead.

"Oh, baby. What have you gone and done? Oh, my sweet baby," Mike murmured as he gazed down at her.

Joanne stood on the other side of her and held her hand as if she were a sleeping child and Joanne was singing her a lullaby. And then, surprisingly, Joanne did start to sing. I finally made out the words to the song: "My Girl" by the Temptations. Her voice had a life energy that made the roots of my hair follicles tingle. Mike started singing with her, and without giving it any thought, I too started singing. The harsh lights changed to an ethereal glow, and tears slid down my cheeks.

△

One day at a time.
12 step program wisdom

Both Mike and I sang and played our guitars at the funeral, harmonizing as if we had played and practiced together for years. We sang "Angel" by Sara McLaughlin. There was a mixture of people attending, young and old, and many people from the rooms of both AA and NA 12 Step programs. Julia had won the hearts of those in attendance and tears gushed like water coming out a drainpipe. Rumor had it that Julia had been involved with an older man who frequented the program with no intentions of finding recovery but rather of manipulating and selling some dope. He had sold or given her heroin cut with fentanyl, a narcotic used to relieve pain for persons with cancer. This product had cut a path down the East Coast, savagely annihilating many souls along the way. As much as I tried to wrap the principles of my 12 Step program around Julia's death, I couldn't seem to do so. Especially, *hope*, the principal behind the second step, [We] "Came to believe that a Power greater than ourselves could restore us to sanity" and *forgiveness*, the principal behind the ninth step, [We] "Made direct amends to such people wherever possible, except when to do so would injure them or others."

I always incorporate a *we* into each step, because I believe, as my sponsor would certainly sanction, that the twelve step program is a *we* program and by myself I could not have found recovery, let alone be willing to work on myself and try and become who I thought my Higher Power intended me to be. Like any belief system, there was always room for different interpretations. This was just how *I* interpreted the literature and my experience in the rooms. Nevertheless, I was enraged and probably would have yielded to its weight and exploded onto this man had I encountered him at that moment.

The 12 Step program emphasized that we should "tell on our disease" and share our emotions behind our desire to use. Whenever I started obsessing about drinking or drugging I needed to tell someone, preferably someone who either understood addiction or even better, was in my positive recovery support network. For me, it was always a good idea to tell on my disease even when I had a passing thought—before I grabbed that thought and starting devising ways to "get away with it" or convincing myself it would be different "this time." My disease would lie to me and tell me that using would take the pain away and I would feel better. That had always been something I struggled with.

My pride didn't want to have to lean on anyone, even if the end result could possibly mean death, or at least my soul dying. Sometimes, the demoralization and living life the complete opposite of one's value system seem as if they might be worse than death. More often than not, that demoralization would at least result in jails and institutions. I remember getting arrested—for public intoxication, driving with no license and possession—for my first time when I was 13. Although my value system was not fully developed, I was already living in a way that my adolescent brain did not approve of even if it rationalized why it was okay.

I was driving because everyone who I was with seemed more fucked up than I was; at least that is what I staunchly believed. Somehow, I had convinced them I was old enough or sober enough to drive. The girl I was hanging around with at that time was 18 years old. She liked to party but couldn't handle her liquor. We had been in the Walmart parking lot, and she had already backed into two parked cars trying to leave. I got behind the wheel, and we took off, never thinking twice about the cars we hit. We picked up some guys somewhere along the way. One of them didn't have a valid driver's license, and the other dude had an outstanding warrant and refused to drive, thinking that was the righteous thing to do even though he let *me* drive—underage, as well as stoned beyond good reason.

I think we had an unfinished orgy of sorts at my "friend" Cindy's apartment before going to

Walmart to get a carton of cigarettes. I just got up in the middle of some heavy petting, half-dressed, and announced I needed a cigarette. It's all kind of fuzzy. We were driving around in a beat-up, old Chevy rusted out in spots that were spray painted a couple of shades lighter green than the car itself, making it look like one of those jackets bought at an army surplus store. We called it our camouflage. Obviously it had not worked because we were arrested later on that day. The authorities could easily spot us. I was wearing cutoff jeans and a bikini top. One of the guys had just painted my toenails all different colors and I was barefoot. I guess I was weaving in and out of traffic. We had swallowed a couple of oxys, finished up the last of our coke, were drinking Mad Dog 20-20 and smoking weed. When I looked in the rearview mirror, I noticed someone trying to flag me over. It was a "paddy wagon," but I thought it was a van filled with people just being friendly. I waved enthusiastically and proceeded on my way. No one else in the car said anything as they were too busy gabbing to notice anything was wrong. Eventually, we were pulled over. It required a roadblock and several police cars to get my attention.

When they took me to jail, I remember bits and pieces about my righteous indignation for my undeserved detainment. I was sputtering and spewing curse words in succession and screamed, "Don't you assholes have anything better to do with your time than fuck with us?" In my delusional thinking, I was sure I was a bad ass, someone they didn't want to mess with.

I dimly remember them finding a bag of pot in my jeans, and my hitting my head on the steel bunk above me when I tried to stand up and yell more obscenities at the passing guard. I must have knocked myself out cold. The humility of waking up with mascara running under my eyes, piss in my pants and puke in my hair while my parents bailed me out is a memory that kind of stays. And there were many of these stories.

When my mom went to court with me for this particular infraction, she insisted that I spend some time in Juvenile Detention when given the option by the courts to either be released to her care or to spend a small chunk of time locked away. To lighten the mood, she even bought me some feety, striped pajamas like the ones that babies wear. She handed them to me as if that would fix everything. Of course the female guard who checked me in confiscated them.

"I have bailed you out long enough. Hopefully, this will get your attention because I can't. I love you, but sometimes that just isn't enough. I don't know what else to do, Rachel." She had tears in her eyes, which I quickly dismissed.

I hissed under my breath as they led me away, "You are one screwed up bitch." I never saw what she was doing as being the right thing to do. I simply could not feel the entirety of my emotions. I writhed with resentment and blame instead.

***

Even though I had made a lot of progress healing from my past and dealing with the loss and the emotions that it evoked, stress triggered me to return to my old habits. I still had a tendency to shut down and focus my attention on everybody or everything else as opposed to what was happening within me. Of course, the end result was that I became moody, impatient and demanding, and I carried around a huge bag of unsatisfied wants that I convinced myself were needs. So when Julia died, I was convinced that all I needed was more time with Mike. I would be the healing salve to spread on his hurt. But Mike needed time alone and more time with his sister to heal. I felt abandoned.

Mike and his sister were in obvious pain. He and Joanne leaned heavily on each other. Mike effectively used the program and his sponsor to help him grieve and mourn his loss as well. I allowed Mike the space to cry, rage and remember. We even started a memorial garden and a scholarship fund in Julia's name. But I was constipated with seething resentment and anger. I had a lot of unrealistic expectations about life, and cringed when it seemed unfair.

My brother, Thomas, came up to see me. He drove from Atlanta, having taken off a week from work to regroup and spend time with his older sister. Thomas loved to hike, fish and do all things outdoors. Asheville, North Carolina, was a perfect place to recharge one's soul. Plus, he seemed to know instinctively that I needed family around.

He stayed with me. I would not think of him staying at the motel when he offered. Thomas knew that I was an introvert. He was afraid he might be intruding on my space. But I was delighted to have him stay with me. Mike breezed in and out as usual and hung out with us on occasion, but stepped aside so Thomas and I could spend some alone time together.

Thomas, who was quick to pick up on my moods, said, "Damn, Rachel . . . you're like an old wood-burning stove with clogged vents that's filling up with smoke."

"What the hell does that mean? Is that some kind of hillbilly lingo I'm supposed to understand?" I said, wanting to be mean for mean's sake.

Thomas had lived in the South a long time and seemed to have "country" embedded in his core. He cherished country cooking, ice tea, do-it-yourself projects and the Panthers football team. And just when friends thought they had him pegged, he would take up writing poetry or invite them to a fire walk, a rite of purification or healing performed by many tribal people as a way to honor fire by walking on burning ash with bare feet. Thomas thought women were angels sent from heaven and really relished their beauty. It didn't matter if they were thin, fat, old or young, he usually could find some redeeming quality in them. I found that fascinating since we both had the same mother. I still had not completely forgiven her or admitted to myself that she, like most everyone, had some wonderful endearing qualities as well as a dark side. I remember she used to take Thomas and me to all things historical—Gettysburg, Pennsylvania; Williamsburg, Virginia; The Alamo in Texas. She made a better tour guide than the tour guides who always related some unknown human interest story that would catch my ear and keep me interested for a minute or two. Thomas loved history more than I did and could retain facts. Eventually, I lost interest in the tour guide's drone and became absorbed by the gardens or any other natural features around whatever place we toured. Either that or I would run off to watch the artisans demonstrate their craft. I practically fell in love with the iron forger at Williamsburg. He had long, dark, curly hair, was dressed up in period clothing with billowing white sleeves and a vest and smiled heartily when I shyly inquired about what he was doing. My mother preferred the historical significance and how it set events into motion. She and Thomas were mystified by my tendency to wander and invariably had to hunt me down wherever I was.

"There you are . . . for Christ sake, Rachel . . . let someone know where you are going," she said more than once in more than a hundred different voices of exasperation.

Secretly I held onto the deluded belief that my mother had loved Thomas exceedingly more than me, which was why he had evoked a more secure sense of self. Thomas always appeared so self-assured on the outside. I had been told to quit comparing my insides to others' outsides by my sponsor, but of course I was not one to listen.

* * *

"I guess I am holding on by a thin thread," I replied to Thomas, trying to smile and erase what I had said. "It has been an emotionally exhausting year. I want to find that son-of-a-bitch who sold Julia that crap! She was just a kid . . . it pisses me off when someone comes into the program and preys on our disease."

"What's the word? Anybody know anything?" Thomas inquired.

"Yeah . . . there is a name floating around. Actually, he may be the same dude who cut a deal with Travis and Brian. Apparently he has connections with some badass people up North. Detective Ross called me and asked a lot of questions. Somehow, I feel responsible, but I am not sure why."

"Sis, this has nothing to do with you," Thomas said with genuine concern in his eyes as he put an arm around me. "It's bigger than you are. Let the authorities sort this out. You need to stay clear of it and focus on your recovery and Mike."

"I have not told Mike anything about the phone call from Detective Ross. I don't know if that is something I should tell him right now. He probably would be pissed if I didn't tell him. But he needs time to heal. I don't know what to do . . . "

"You are probably right, Mike would be pissed if you didn't tell him. Rachel, it isn't your burden to carry alone. Mike needs to know what is going on. He is a big boy," Thomas emphasized, "and probably a lot stronger than you give him credit for."

Later that evening, Thomas, as a support, went with me to an open speaker's meeting. At an open speaker's meeting, the attendees do not have to declare themselves addicts or alcoholics. This is the meeting that family and friends of alcoholics and addicts usually go to or those not convinced that they suffer from the disease of addiction. A person does not have to introduce himself or herself like at a discussion meeting and can slip out unnoticed if that is the intention. I tried to listen to the speaker but found myself searching the room for anyone who looked like he or she didn't belong . . . as if I would know what that looked like. At some point or the other, most of us feel we don't belong even "in the rooms" (as it is commonly called). So, it seemed absurd that I thought I could pick out such a person in a crowd.

Thomas stuck his finger in my ear, something he used to do when we were young, and it brought me back into focus. He laughed as I jumped. I looked at him with a face full of irritation, which quickly dissolved as I saw the huge grin he wore. And in that moment, all the resentment and envy I had nursed regarding him dissipated. I grinned back at him with tears in my eyes and said, "God, I didn't realize how much I missed you in my life."

He hugged me, and I hugged back without reserve. The rest of his visit was cathartic. We laughed and shared a lifetime of what we missed. We hiked up to Mount Mitchell and yelled obscenities at the top. We barbecued ribs and invited Joanne and Mike over. Thomas taught me to shag. We were caught up in a "bad joke" marathon, and I laughed so hard I peed in my pants, which made everyone else laugh even harder. When Thomas packed his belongings to leave the next morning, I cried. I did not want him to leave.

"Rachel, this has been as good for me as it was for you, believe me. I lost you once; I won't let that happen again."

Satchmo and I chased him down the driveway, saying our goodbyes. I hated to see him go.

The next day, I told Mike about the call from Detective Ross. He listened attentively and afterward he said with a sigh, "More will be revealed, I suppose."

* * *

The following weekend, I went to a meeting with Mike. A mutual friend was picking up her ten-year chip. The usual group was hanging outside, smoking cigarettes before the meeting. I heard a familiar voice. I peered into the crowd to see where it was coming from. Much to my surprise, I picked Becca out. She spotted me just as I spotted her.

"Oh my God! I never thought I would see you here . . . oh my God! God is good . . ." I cried, pulling her to me in an embrace that might have broken her ribs if I hadn't let go when I did.

Before she could say anything, she started sobbing. I hugged her again, this time a little more gently and continued until her breathing became more even and she stopped crying.

Mike stood off to the side quietly. That was another quality I loved about him, his ability to allow people their moment without being invasive or judgmental. He gave off the air of simple acceptance.

I introduced Mike, who indicated he was going inside to help set up the tables and chairs. We were early. I was glad because it allowed time for me to talk to Becca.

Becca shared what brought her to the rooms with no pretense.

"I got busted. But that didn't stop me. You know me... have to do things the hard way," she gushed with tears welling up in her eyes. "I got mixed up with a nasty bunch of folks and got the shit kicked out of me. Put me in the hospital. The doctors didn't think I'd make it. Was in intensive care for over two weeks. But that wasn't near as bad as what was going on in my head. I thank God every day for a new beginning . . . oh my stars, seeing you here is a blessing. You look so good. Oh, girl, it is so good to see you!"

I felt something. I wasn't really sure what it was; it felt so warm and tender like a mother's hand touching her baby's cheek for the first time. I knew instinctively it was my God making sure I paid attention. I was filled with gratitude, unconditional love and, I guess, grace.

I remember studying *Religions of Man* as an elective in undergraduate school. I read with emotional detachment man's experience with the spiritual realm. I did not trust or believe in any Supreme Being and courted melancholy and skepticism obsessively. And even though I had felt gratitude and a taste of serenity once or twice since I started my journey in recovery, this was the first time I allowed the experience its chance without thinking it to death.

"Sit with me, Becca. I've got a whole slew of people I want you to meet. I don't want you to feel overwhelmed, but these folks would make a coyote feel welcome . . . not that you are a mongrel . . . oh, I need to shut up," I rambled as I grabbed her hand and pulled her inside.

Becca howled as only she could.

"Well, I guess that's why I thought of a coyote," I said, laughing with her.

I introduced Becca to my sponsor and anyone and everyone I could think of who had quality sobriety and "walked the walk," as they emphasized, not just "talked the talk." She already knew a few of them. Becca indicated she had gone to meetings for a while on the other side of town but recently relocated closer to where I usually went to meetings.

"I decided that if I was going to start over, I needed to start over. I am back in school at AB Tech, got a Pell Grant, work part-time and go to a ton of meetings. I got accepted into nursing school, believe it or not. I have lots of experience with pharmaceuticals . . ." she trailed off as the meeting got started. I looked at her with a smile and she winked.

Mike sat nearby and smiled tenderly at me when I looked back at him. His eyes conveyed how genuinely happy he was that Becca had found her way to the rooms. I felt a love so complete I was certain that if my life ended right at that moment, I would not have any reason to complain.

Of course, as with all feelings, it passed. I suppose it's human nature to complicate most things, but this addict's brain could complicate a summer day given half a chance. I wondered if Satchmo ever complicated anything. Then I laughed to myself, knowing that as long as he had food, water, could run like the wind and had someone to scratch behind his ears, he was happy. Maybe Satchmo did relish in simple pleasures, but that seemed very wise to me somehow.

Becca asked my sponsor's sponsor to be *her* sponsor, keeping it all in the family. She easily fit into my positive recovery-support group. Some people say that having used together can be a negative influence; it can trigger a desire to "pick up." Since the American Society of Addiction Medicine bases its definition of addiction on a biopsychosocial model, meaning there are biological, psychological and social factors involved, it was already imprinted in my memory that I had used with Becca, and this might involuntarily produce a craving, which in turn might spark a compulsion to use. I use the analogy of cookies baking. When we smell them baking, the aroma makes us want one, and it doesn't seem to matter that we are dieting or if we have diabetes. It just happens. But Becca wasn't asking me to be her sponsor, and neither of us glorified the drug and alcohol history we had together. Our continued interaction seemed to work. And I was learning to be grateful when things worked.

* * *

Life returned to its daily hum. I went to work and thrived. I even earned a merit raise. Mike continued to grieve, but it was with quiet grace. Our relationship seemed to go to a deeper level. He was very sensual, and our lovemaking left me breathless. We connected spiritually, and our journey led us by the hand to an intimacy I had never before experienced. That did not mean we didn't allow our fears to take center stage, but we didn't stay there as long as in days past. We both were making progress.

It was the everyday irritations we squabbled about. Mike didn't always eat healthy and would snack on Little Debbie cakes. This infuriated me because I wanted to gorge on them as well when they were in the house. But I didn't want him to know that. So I sneaked around and, sometimes standing up, ate them, two or three at a time. Then I would blame him for my lack of discipline. Whenever I did this, I believed I had gained twenty pounds in this moment of excess and obsessively exercised and ate practically nothing for a couple of days. This ritual threw me head-first down my dark hole of self-loathing. Intellectually, it felt ridiculous, which made me hate myself more.

"Let me feel that little belly," Mike would tease. I instinctively wanted to cover it up and felt he was judging it critically because it was not washboard flat. At 5' 6" I weighed 120 pounds even on my bloated, premenstrual, don't-dare-look-at-me days, but in my mind I still struggled with my body image.

Sometimes Mike made random, spontaneous comments about a woman—on television or in a movie—who was scantily clad. Nothing too rude or crude, but just a male remark appreciating the wonders of a well-put-together female body, and I verbally assaulted him in my mind. Occasionally it escaped and came out my mouth.

"Women aren't possessions to be ogled," I would spit. "You are just like most men . . . all you think about is tits and ass and nothing else!"

Mike always looked confused like a stray dog at the humane society, and I would immediately apologize.

Mike knew bits and pieces of my past, including my sexual abuse. I had shared more with him than I had ever shared with anyone other than with my sponsor during my Fourth Step. But on those "bad self-esteem days," as I called them, I still obsessed that if he knew all of me, he would run away screaming into the night. But most days I felt confident in his love for me.

Fall was in full swing, with the leaves shouting colors so vividly that we knew the Blue Ridge Parkway was a clear testimony to God's artistic genius. Spring was my favorite season, but fall was a close second. I took delight in the crisp, clean air and the sound the leaves made as we walked on them. Mike had planned for us to go to Brevard, North Carolina, to an outdoor venue celebrating folk music and local musicians. Afterward, we went to a wonderful restaurant with a collection of delightful aromas filling its dining room. It was located right in the heart of this quaint town. As we sat waiting for our desserts to arrive, Mike pulled out a little velvet box and sat it in front of me.

"You make my life complete. I thought I was content before I met you, but since you came into my life, I have felt things I have never felt and have grown in ways I might never have grown. I love you with all of me. Rachel, I will get down on my knees in front of all of these strangers if that would make you happy. Will you do me the honor and become my wife?" Mike spoke tenderly, his eyes gazing into mine.

"I ... um ... I ... um," I stuttered breathlessly. I had not seen this coming. "I love you, too. And yes, I would be honored to become your wife," I said, pulling myself together. I opened the box and saw a unique, vintage-looking diamond ring made of white gold. I gasped.

"I had this handmade by a local artist from Mother's ring," Mike said. "It had been Julia's idea. She knew I would marry you long before I did." And with that we both started crying just as the waiter was bringing our desserts. The waiter had such an odd look on his face it was hard to tell if he thought he might not get a good tip, or he actually felt a moment of compassion and curiosity. Both Mike and I, after seeing his face, started to laugh with the tears still wet on our faces.

"Is everything all right?" The waiter hesitantly asked as if he were talking to a family member with a history of psychotic breaks.

"I just asked this beautiful creature to marry me, and she said yes!" Mike practically shouted, smiling broadly as if he just learned he had won front row tickets to his favorite rock band. "I didn't even have to get down on these creaky knees to get the answer I wanted."

"Oh, well, that is wonderful! In that case, the dessert is on the house!" the waiter responded, looking relieved.

* * *

The next morning was Sunday. While Mike lay in my bed with his legs tangled up in the sheets, I carefully removed his forearm that lay draped over my chest and padded to the adjoining bathroom. I had not removed the ring and stared down at it after finishing my morning rituals. Suddenly, as if someone had punched me in the stomach, I felt like all the air had been knocked out of me and a panic invaded my body.

I looked up at the mirror. My eyes had a look I imagined a young buck might have when it realized a hunter had been stalking him and heard the crack of the rifle as it released a bullet aiming for its heart.

I started obsessing about life with Mike, and even though I loved him dearly, I was consumed with fear. I couldn't extract my reasons for this fear. It seemed as elusive as the motives behind a psychopath's rage.

And just for that moment, I wanted to get high. Because I had been doing the work that was essential to maintain sobriety, I knew instinctively what to do. First I prayed, and then I picked up the phone and called my sponsor.

"Hello?" Debbie answered sleepily.

Satchmo had followed me into the living room and sat alert at my feet as I spoke into my cell phone. "Hey, it's me. I need to talk. You got a moment?" I inquired. The urgency in my voice was giving me away.

"Of course, sweetie. What's up? You sound panicky."

"Mike proposed to me last night. He gave me a beautiful ring. I accepted," I blurted. My words seemed to trip on one another.

"And?" Debbie questioned.

"I want to get so fucked up I don't see the light of day!" I cried.

Debbie had a way of pulling me out of myself without being overly critical while interjecting hope at the same time. She knew the 12 steps like she knew her own face. And her spiritual self was her constant companion.

I shared all the self-doubt that was in my head as quickly and succinctly as I could, knowing if I didn't tell on my disease, it would take its iron claw and pull out my heart.

It took almost an hour to exorcise my demons. But, in the end, I was able to laugh at myself and felt as if I were ten pounds lighter.

"I owe you a Starbucks," I promised before hanging up.

I looked down at Satchmo, who had given up his sentry post and had sprawled out on the rug.

I heard Mike's usual morning noises echoing off the bedroom walls. He had a habit of moaning several times and then repeating his quick prayer of gratitude, "Thank you, God, for another day," out loud as if God were hard of hearing.

"Baby, where are you? Satchmo? Come keep me company!" he implored. Mike and Satchmo had become buddies. Satchmo's ears picked up and he cocked his head to one side. Then he practically skated into the bedroom and jumped on the bed.

I listened as he and Mike tussled on the bed. It seemed so natural and it made me smile.

I decided right then and there I didn't need to share my moment of insanity with him, as it would serve no purpose. I got up and crept back in the bed with him; I joined in on the merriment, and we both played with Satchmo for another half hour before we got up to start the day.

"It's kind of chilly in here," Mike said. "I'm going to build a fire." Mike started a nice fire as I made omelets and homemade pumpkin pancakes. Fall and pumpkins were synonymous in my opinion. So Mike got to be the taste-tester for all things pumpkin—scrumptious pumpkin muffins and pumpkin pancakes. But the pumpkin bisque was horrific. It was a good thing Mike didn't complain much, or I might have been a little testy.

* * *

Later that day, while Mike watched his favorite college football team, Texas A&M, on television, Detective Ross called. I answered the phone.

"I've got a lead on this character who we think is pushing this batch of bad heroin," he reported. "He is definitely part of a bigger group of hustlers who have runners over the entire southern part of the country. They hail from Cleveland, Ohio. Apparently, he tried to get clean at a methadone clinic there and got contracted out due to dirty urines. He met another character there who was also not interested in recovery that knew another guy and so on. So, he knows the drill and where to look for vulnerable buyers."

"Is there anything I can do?" I questioned.

"Just look out for him and let me know if you hear anything. His nickname is 'Red.' He's in his thirties, has auburn hair and freckles and has one of those baby faces that say trust me just as he's slamming an ice pick in your back! He apparently sold a load of goodies to Brian. He is able to get his hands on heroin, meth and crack . . . whatever the market calls for. But he's using a shit load of the stuff himself, which makes him pretty volatile. Be careful," Detective Ross warned.

I hung up the phone quietly and joined Mike on the couch.

"Who was that, baby? Mike asked.

"Detective Ross." I said matter-of-factly.

Mike turned and looked me. "And?" he asked in a little-too-loud voice.

I relayed what the detective had shared, interjecting as little emotion as I could. I did not want to trigger any unnamed reactive anger from Mike. I was not sure I would be able to provide the comfort he might need.

"That son-of-a-bitch better not show his face at any meeting I go to!" Mike spewed. "I am not sure that God's grace would save his freckled ass!"

I flinched as if he had hit me. Instinctively, his voice softened and he said, "Rachel, I know that would not help anything. Saying it and doing it are two different things. I'll spread the word. If he comes back around, we will call the authorities and let them deal with it, okay?"

"Yeah, he wouldn't want a bunch of us crazies whooping up on him!" I said, laughing hysterically.

We held each other, and one thing led to another. Ah, the healing power of touch . . . As usual we had to shoo Satchmo away or he would just sit there and watch. "Get out of here, you pervert!" Mike bellowed. Satchmo startled and ran off into the other room.

Mike packed up his things to return to the little cabin he owned. I always felt sad when he left. Even though he was practically living with me full time, periodically he would leave for a couple of days to check on his house.

"We need to put my cabin up for sale and decide if we want to remodel your house or sell it and buy us a new house. We need to come up with a wedding date so you can become the little missus," he kidded. He knew that would set me off on one of my women's-lib tangents.

"I'm not going to be anyone's little missus, buddy-rum. If you think I am going to cook and clean for you because it's my duty, you better re-think that," I quipped, knowing full well Mike didn't think that at all.

Mike left and I was left to sit bare-naked in my thoughts. There was nothing to distract me. As usual, I would philosophize out loud to Satchmo, who would follow me dutifully around from room to room as I talked and cleaned. Cleaning and making things "pretty" always made me feel better. It was the only thing I seemed to have any control over.

I fantasized about different scenarios where I would run into this same dude whom I blamed for Julia's death and how I would single-handedly serve him my brand of justice—ridiculous plots where I was a cross between Wonder Woman, Hillary Clinton and the main female character in the novel, *The Girl with the Dragon Tattoo*. I laughed at my own creative genius as Satchmo looked up at me with eyes that said, "You are as Looney Tunes as it gets!"

I did have the afterthought that I ought not only to call my sponsor, but also to get out of my head and call and check up on Becca. I was exercising what I had been taught, that the best way to get out of my head was to help someone else.

After talking with my sponsor and getting "right-sized," I called Becca.

"Hidey Ho, stranger!" I chimed into the phone.

"Oh, gosh, what a coincidence . . . I was just thinking of you," Becca replied. "I have had a week of exams, which is now thankfully over. I wanted to celebrate. And no, not with drugs and alcohol. Maybe a frappe and a piece of cake though. Are you up for it? I'd like to see that pretty face of yours and talk recovery."

"Yeah, sounds good. Sundays are a good day to hang out with the ones you love. Mike left a couple hours ago to do some stuff at his cabin.

Satchmo and I were just puttering around the house. I was spending way too much time in my head!"

We met at a little coffee shop in West Asheville. It harbored a bunch of works of art that were really eclectic, leaning toward the bizarre. The owners made great frappes and gluten-free, chocolate-chip, pumpkin muffins. Not that I really cared much about being gluten free, but it tasted great, so if it was considered healthier, I thought that was a good deal.

Becca actually seemed to glow. Her skin was flawless and her eyes held a clarity that I had not ever seen, as if she could see beyond what *was* to what *could* be. We talked about gratitude, building a relationship with our Higher Power, her school and the 12 Steps. Becca was like those of us who took recovery beyond just putting down the substance. She used it to change her life, to transform her way of thinking and to practice it "in all her affairs." So, it meant taking a daily inventory, making amends promptly and making a conscious decision to quit obsessing about people, places and things that created havoc in her life.

"I started to freak out about my grades and interacting with other students," she related as she broke pieces of cake off and nibbled on them. "I tended to judge myself by who I thought *they* were, based on how they looked and acted."

I just listened and tried to be present.

"Occasionally, I would start to obsess how much easier it would be just to tune out and give up . . . you know . . . drink and drug away how insecure I felt. But, 'cause I have been busting a gut trying to do what you people and my sponsor tell me to do, I knew instinctively that was bullshit! So I called my sponsor and worked the first three steps:

    I can't,

    My Higher Power can, and

    I am going to let her.

"I like to think my Higher Power is a female," she said and then started to snicker.

△

Let go and let God.
12 step program wisdom

MEN HAD SEXUALLY and physically abused both Becca and me in our childhoods. In the Big Book, the repeated reference to the male gender and inference that the Higher Power was male would sometimes cause our skin to recoil and our resentments to flare. But it was something that we could talk about, and the general inference in the rooms was that we could interpret our Higher Power to be what our Higher Power needed to be at any given time.

After over an hour of sharing with authentic intensity, Becca asked me about Julia's death.

She talked about her last high—getting beat-up and landing in the hospital. Becca wondered out loud if the people who did that to her might have been indirectly related to Julia's death.

"If you think that is the case, Becca, please call Detective Ross," I interjected.

Becca looked down at her plate for what seemed like a long time. When she looked up, her glow had turned into a pasty-color. Her eyes were filled with fear the color of nightfall, and she said, "I'm afraid to, Rachel. They tried to kill me." She hung her head and tears dropped down on her empty plate.

My heart swelled with compassion for my dear friend. At the same time, I felt a sense of justifiable anger swell up inside my brain. I fidgeted with the ring on my finger, took a breath and said, "I am sure we can get some support to help you walk through this thing. And we can be like Siamese twins if you need it."

We agreed to talk to our sponsors. I would talk with Mike and my brother, Thomas. She would talk to the detective. It was understood that we would be with her when she made that call or met in person with Detective Ross.

As I drove away, the Carolina blue sky seemed more ominous than welcoming. Instead of enjoying the symphony of sounds birds produced, I was more reminded of the Hitchcock movie, *Birds* and was fixated on the stray black crow I saw. This was not making my driving too safe. I almost ran into another car that stopped in front of me in order to turn. Impending doom coursed through my body like an intravenous saline solution. I tried to identify my feeling. It was fear.

The 12 Step acronym for fear, FACE EVERYTHING AND RECOVER seemed to lose its significance. Instead FUCK EVERYTHING AND RUN stuck its ragged talons in me. These were phrases I'd always heard at meetings, but now they took on real meaning, like having a miscarriage, not just reading about it.

It beckoned me to pull up a chair and stay a spell. Instead, I put on my favorite uplifting, hard-hitting gospel music and turned it up so the car was a moving music studio. Afterward, I called Debbie, picked up Satchmo and drove to Bent Creek to go hiking. I was starting to utilize my tools of recovery even if I did stop at McDonald's en route and order a preservative-filled, sugar-laden frappe!

I liked to drive the gravel roads into the thick of the woods and hike one of the longer trails that dipped and curved its way around the rhododendron and mountain pines. Satchmo could run unencumbered by a leash. Debbie brought her dog, Rufus, part German Shepherd and Collie, whom Satchmo loved. They danced and whizzed around each other like hummingbirds around a feeder. At first we just walked and absorbed the quiet of the woods. I loved the pea green moss that cradled the hard rock, the sound our feet made when they walked over hard dirt and root, and the whisper of a mountain stream gurgling somewhere deep inside the wood's folds.

"So, what are you are afraid is going to happen?" Debbie blurted out as we half-trotted down a steeper part of the trail, trying to regain our footing.

My mind seemed to regain it's footing as well. I was not that good at pinpointing my fears. They seemed to hover like fireflies and then zip off somewhere else.

"I don't know, plain and simple," I answered, not sure where I was going with this train of thought. "I am just afraid something horrible will happen and that I won't be able to stop it or that maybe my involvement will make it worse than it needs to be . . ."

"That seems to be generalized fear and anxiety as if something from yesterday makes you think crap is inevitable today." Debbie declared. Her words seemed to reverberate off the tree bark.

"I am not sure I know what you are trying to say. My life seems to have been a series of short stories where everyone dies in the end . . . no feel good story line for me," I responded out of habit, knowing when I said it that it was a lie. I used to think it was the truth. Now, most days, I no longer accepted it as my truth. I winced at how quickly I could resort to old thinking. I apologized and quickly added,". . . until I got clean and started to realize just how lucky I have been and didn't even know it."

"Wow, Rachel, you are growing up. So let's figure this thing out. The way I see it, we need to be there for Becca. And then, there is Julia. How can we better commemorate her loss than to stand up for her and ask that justice be served? I am not talking about that 'justifiable anger' they speak about in the Big Book, which has a tendency to set us up to fail. Then we are demanding things to go our way and refuse to accept anything else. I am just talking about doing the next right thing. Go home and discuss it with Mike and his sister and we will take it from there. Right now, let's just enjoy our time with the dogs and this glorious day."

Debbie had a way of clarifying things for me. I could muddle up and complicate a peanut butter and jelly sandwich. This was one of those times I was more than glad she was my sponsor.

We kept hiking as the sun played hide-and-go-seek between the trees. A squirrel, oblivious to what was about to happen once the dogs noticed it, was chasing its tail at the base of a tree. It flopped and hopped like a rabbit. I smiled. Just as my lips upturned, Satchmo, spotted it. He ran full sprint at the squirrel like a pellet from a BB gun. He was fast, but the squirrel was faster and took off up the tree. Satchmo strained on his hind legs with his fore paws braced against the trunk, glaring up into the top of the tree as the squirrel, seeming to mock him, jumped from branch to branch in slow motion.

It was times like these, so simple but full, that I felt glad to be alive . . . and present.

When Mike came home, as soon as I heard him step out of his car, I ran out to embrace him, arms outstretched like one of those military wives welcoming their soldier home.

We stood there for a while as I absorbed his energy and the smell of him, and my whole body seemed to relax. He murmured into the nape of my neck, "God, I love you." I felt awestruck by the blessings that were in my life. It seemed weird to me that I should be so fortunate. Not to say that I allowed myself to feel this on a consistent basis, but I was starting to have these moments more often.

We walked hand in hand in the front door, and Satchmo, with his backside waggling back and forth, almost knocked Mike down welcoming him home.

Mike beamed. "I should leave more often . . . sure feels good coming home!"

I helped Mike unpack. We chatted about the realtor he had contacted and the process of putting his cabin up for sale. Mike indicated that although he was looking forward to our life together, he was going to miss his little cabin in the woods. We both commiserated about how it would be nice to keep if we could afford it, but agreed we could not and moved on to more inane conversation.

After a while, I brought up the subject of Becca and Julia. Whenever I mentioned Julia, I noticed Mike's eyes still clouded over, and it made me sad.

"I agree with Debbie. We will do what needs to be done. I want to see whoever had their hands in this—" he stopped as if to collect his thoughts and his emotions, "—be put away for a long time." I knew instinctively that Mike still harbored some bottled-up rage that he was trying to turn over and my heart went out to him. He would never act on that rage, and eventually he would find a way to give it to God. This I was certain. But it was a process.

We made love that night with a new level of abandon and intimacy that almost healed my broken mind. Almost. Like Mike, I had some bottled up rage that I hadn't turned over. But I was starting to believe that maybe in time I would.

The next day, we finished our morning routines and went to work. My job filled a part of me that needed filling. I was in my element. I knew I couldn't fix everyone, but I damn sure could be present and was able to pull out some hope in creative ways. I knew that I was able to tap into that God-given gift better than before, now that I was in recovery.

Crystal, a redhead with freckles adorning her body like stars in the night sky, was broken. She was 17 and pregnant. All her immediate family was caught in their own trap of addiction and she was alone. Her child was a product of a rape.

"Crystal, if a genie came and gave you three wishes what would they be? " I asked.

"Oh . . . I dunno . . . uh . . . well, that I had all the money in the world and never had to ask anyone for help. Then I could buy my mom a home of her own so she didn't have to live in housing . . ."

Crystal had a habit of biting at her cuticles when she was nervous and was doing so now. I didn't interrupt or start talking when there was this huge chunk of silence. I waited.

". . . and be able to get her treatment . . ."

She looked down at her hands, took a breath and continued.

"I would want my baby to be healthy and loved by everyone even if she is, you know, made by hate . . ."

She sighed loudly as if she didn't believe she was saying it out loud.

"And I would want to be turned beautiful."

Everything in me wanted to cry, but I didn't. She was such an amazing, strong, compassionate women-child. On top of that, she had a creative artistic gift. After the sharing of the three wishes, we tapped into that and made a collage of this vision that would make Rembrandt jealous. Or so I thought later. I took it and had it framed and gift-wrapped and gave it back to her when she left it in my office. She then, in a moment of total unselfishness, tried to give it to me. I knew we were not supposed to take gifts, and told her so. We decided to hang it in our office lobby instead, and she cried like a baby.

Gratitude, although fleeting at times, was important in my recovery. I knew that sometimes these insights had been realized many times before, but each time I read them they seemed to have a deeper meaning and I was able to apply them more effectively. *It's somewhat like superglue*, I thought. *I have to put just the right amount and apply just the right amount of pressure for it to take hold.* Then I laughed out loud at my analogy, looking around quickly afterward to make sure no one took notice lest they think I was becoming unglued.

A couple of weeks later, I received another phone call while I was sitting on my couch and eating popcorn with Satchmo, watching reruns of my favorite sitcom, *Everybody Loves Raymond.* I ate a few pieces and then threw a piece in the air to see if Satchmo could catch it. You can't throw popcorn with much accuracy, so Satchmo wasn't too successful catching it, and it made me laugh watching him try. Mike was mowing the yard. Even though I had been halfway expecting the telephone call, I still wasn't good at responding to life and tended to react first, regroup and then respond. Sometimes, it called for an amends because of my inability to think it through, breathe and not fall back on old thinking.

* * *

Detective Ross would clear his throat at the beginning of a conversation almost intentionally as a way of establishing who was in charge. It was slightly annoying on one hand, but comforting on the other, so I wasn't surprised when I felt a pinch of *irritation* creeping up my spine paired with its unlikely twin *security* following close behind as I heard his deep baritone command my attention.

"We have talked to your friend and pieced together enough evidence that the DA thinks we have a case. The heroin that killed Julia was higher quality than what is usually seen around here. We want to charge this character with contributing to the delinquency of a minor, which resulted in her death. Because of his connection to a pretty fair-sized drug-smuggling operation, we do have some concerns about yours and Becca's welfare. We will be placing you both under surveillance and if anything, anything at all seems out of the ordinary, you are to call me at once."

I asked a couple of questions relating to the matter and then burst into tears. It turned out that I knew the defendant and had actually bought drugs from him myself. "Scramble" as his associates called him, hung out a lot with Brian. He was in and out of the rooms and had picked up numerous white chips, tokens to symbolize his willingness to work the 12 Step program. I was never convinced of his sincerity, but who was I to judge? He had blown into town periodically through the last years of my using. I had seen him on the street and at meetings.

A side of Detective Ross came out I had not experienced. The tone of his voice changed like the Gulf Stream. It became almost like liquid and flowed. "Rachel, we won't let anything happen to either of you. You have my personal promise."

It was so reassuring and soothing that I stopped crying almost at once. Satchmo seemed to recognize I was in distress and had come to lie at my feet and put his head on my foot. Somehow, I knew then that it would be all right.

△

Acceptance is the answer to all my problems today.
12 step program wisdom

The trial was set in slow motion. It did seem to take longer than I thought it should. It was postponed for a long while simply because the court docket was a bureaucratic nightmare. I would shift from periods of being so busy I seemed to forget about it looming in the background, to having what Mike dubbed a "crapitude," which didn't mean I was filled with light and love.

"Would you please quit leaving your nail clippers on the kitchen counter? For Christ sake, people eat there," I chastised. "And why the hell can't you please turn off the bathroom light after you use the toilet? We all are responsible for conserving energy."

It was completely out of the blue. No warning. I took my aim and fired.

Mike appeared a little anxious himself. He went fishing more often at the little pond a friend of his owned, and he ate copious amounts of Ben and Jerry's ice cream. Luckily he worked out a lot or we would have had to buy him a whole new wardrobe. Satchmo seemed oblivious to the stirrings and his need for daily walks and feedings kept us to a "sort of routine," which helped. We also went to a lot of 12 Step program and NA meetings and volunteered with "Bridging the Gap," a program that connected an addict or alcoholic when discharged from in-patient treatment to 12 Step meetings.

So, we decided to plan our wedding sooner than later. We felt that the distraction would be good for the soul, and since it was supposed to be a celebration of our love, we did not factor in the stress. Of course our addict brains floated on the river of denial occasionally still. So off we went . . .

Mike declared, "I will be happy with anything as long as you are happy. I live to serve you," he said with a lopsided smile and a glint in his eye. But then, he seemed to have a lot of loud opinions when it came to the planning. I couldn't tell if he was seriously interested or just wanted to bait me, which fueled my tendency to complicate it, be more fickle than decisive and want to chunk it all and get married by the Justice of the Peace.

My dear friends stepped in and plans were set into motion like a paper airplane drifting off a balcony. A friend of a friend—who was a wonderful seamstress with a creative talent so huge people were on a waiting list for her nimble fingers to stitch, embroider and imagine a one-of-a-kind miracle—agreed to make me a delightful calf-length dress, regardless of who came before me on the list.

"I remember going to the NA convention and you were giving your talk," the seamstress recounted. "You said that you had relapsed and really were not sure why you had been asked to speak. I remember that you only had a year of what you said was good recovery,"

"Yeah, and I was so nervous. I thought everyone there who was speaking *must* have better quality recovery than I did. I was still squirming around in shame."

"Well, it really helped me. I had relapsed and only had three days clean when I heard you speak. I felt sordid and dirty and would have gone back out I think if I hadn't heard your talk. It gave me hope and turned my life around. I have been clean ever since and never looked back."

"Wow . . ." I stuttered, ". . . um, I feel honored. I am sure glad I resisted my urge to say no when they asked me to talk . . ."

My dream dress was repurposed from antique dresses and embellishments she had collected. She even embroidered a silk "Russian Firebird" in crème colored thread with hints of aqua and magenta so subtle I had to really pay attention to see it.

I had made the drawing from a series of plates handed down to me from my father telling the Russian Fairy Tale. The Firebird in the account my father told is an object of a difficult quest. It is a beautiful bird, which is highly coveted and eventually captured. But because of the hardships encountered, ultimately the Firebird itself is blamed for all the adversity anyone stumbled upon trying to capture its beauty.

The dress was the most stunning article of clothing I had ever seen. It fit my body perfectly, accentuating all my curves.

I found some satin "almost" ballet slippers that did not detract from the dress and were as comfortable to wear as bedroom slippers. Originally, I had considered buying a new pair of Rocket Dog tennis shoes that were beyond colorful, just to annoy Mike because he always chided me when I wore the ones I already owned, saying they looked like "clown shoes." But pretty won out. Since I had a tendency to be slightly clumsy in heels, even though I had the legs for them some said, I opted for understated, practical, but pretty.

I wore a sterling silver necklace I had made with bits of turquoise and coral. It had a silver, hand-forged bird—that a silversmith friend made years before—hanging from it on an O-ring. It fit the dress perfectly and brought attention to my neckline, which was daring for me but probably not for anyone else.

My long tresses were curled in loose ringlets, with part of my hair braided off my forehead and adorned with wildflowers that matched my bouquet. I felt like a Russian princess and wanted to twirl round and round and sing the only Russian folk song I knew:

Beriozka (The Birch Tree) or
In the Field Stood a Birch Tree.

See the lovely birch in the meadow,
Curly leaves all dancing when the wind blows
Loo-lee-loo, when the wind blows,
Loo-lee-loo, when the wind blows.

Oh, my little tree, I need branches,
For the silver flutes I need branches.
Loo-lee-loo, three branches,
Loo-lee-loo, three branches.

From another birch I will make now,
I will make a tingling balalaika.
Loo-lee-loo, balalaika,
Loo-lee-loo, balalaika.

When I play my new balalaika,
I will think of you, my lovely birch tree.
Loo-lee-loo, lovely birch tree,
Loo-lee-lee, lovely birch tree.

My father used to sing this song when he was working on his stamp collection in his study. Sometimes when I was little, I tiptoed and slid into a corner adjacent to the door where he could not see me and listened. It still makes my eyes tear up when I recall his melodious deep voice and the sense of comfort it brought me as I sat unnoticed in that alcove.

As I was walking toward Mike, I could feel a longing wrap around my heart, wishing my father were there to give me away. My iridescent green eyes shined with romanticism, sentiment and a few glistening tears as I resisted my urge to dance uninhibited like a child.

We had decided to get married at Chimney Rock Park with the mountains as our backdrop. Mike wore a classic tuxedo with an aqua bow tie. His silly side had him wearing aqua colored Keds, high top tennis shoes. I wished I had worn my Rocket Dogs after all and, for a second, a spot of resentment tried to spread itself out in my head. But my heart ruled it out. It just melted when I saw him standing in front, waiting for me with tears in his eyes and a grin on his face. We had reserved a chair for Julia. On it sat a framed picture of her. Wild flowers were everywhere. Friends had pulled together an amazing band that was just starting to get off the ground, but we knew they would someday be big. Mike and I wrote our own vows, and they seemed to reverberate into the chorus of bird sounds that filled the air. My brother gave me away. We dubbed Maija my "Matron of Honor" due to her advancing years. She was absolutely stunning in an aqua and cream suit with her salt and pepper hair framing her face like a halo. Even though I had not always found the time to visit with her outside work, she was still a huge part of my life, and I considered her the mother I thought I never had.

There were the usual miscalculations; we did not have enough chairs for the attendees. And Satchmo, adorned with his own aqua bowtie, would not be still and wanted to greet everyone and pee on everything, but it was perfect in its imperfection.

At the covered pavilion, we danced our first dance as man and wife to "That's Where It's At," an old R&B classic by Sam Cooke. Mike brought a CD with that song on it to Charleston when we first made love, and I knew then it was the beginning. We had danced to it in the privacy of our room, with lights turned down low. He still sings it to me in a guttural voice when he is moved to do so as he did on this special day. It was like it was just him and me out there on the floor, and I felt almost giddy. An old haunting voice tried to come out of the shadows to warn me of things unseen, but the beauty and grace of the moment dropkicked it out my head.

"You are absolutely stunning . . . and I am the luckiest man in the world," Mike whispered to me. Even though I thought he probably said those words because he knew I'd like to hear them, I still liked hearing them.

Fortunately, Mike sold his cabin. We had decided to live in my house, at least for the time being. Mike was an excellent woodworker, so we figured that together, with my creativity and his skills, we could make my house ours. Mike had a lot of patience and took time to teach me how to build things and use his power tools with no trace of the condescending undertone some men might have. For this I was grateful.

We honeymooned in Bali with some of the money accrued from the sale of his home. Mike had booked us a room at the Bulgary Hotel in the Nusa Dura Region. It was absolutely regal by my standards. We went to the Monkey Forest in the

Kuta region and the Baruna Dive Center. Mike and I had taken scuba diving lessons to prepare for our trip. Still, I was a little scared. I remembered that our dive instructor was always poking fun at me during our class. "I still see one little mermaid's hiney poking up out of the water!" He would chortle out loud.

I struggled trying to learn how to breathe and submerge at the same time. Secretly, I wanted to punch him in the head whenever he amused himself at my expense. But I smiled instead as I glared at him like the hot summer sun reflecting off a glass skyscraper in a big city. Still, we managed to get our certificates despite my buoyancy. During the whole experience, except at the very end, I harbored a hidden obsessive concern that if I did not remember what I needed to do and panicked and my equipment malfunctioned, Mike might not share his breathing apparatus with me. So here we were living the dream. Once I let go of my fear, the beauty and pure magnificence of our diving experience in Bali could not be put into words.

We also witnessed the Barong, a storytelling dance, which epitomized the fight between good, and evil. Barong is a character in the mythology of Bali. He is the good spirit and Rangda is the bad spirit. Actually, Barong is thought of as a protector and is often represented as a lion just as in this dance. I am an August baby: Leo the lion. It seemed beyond coincidental to me. All my life was that dance between good and evil. And I was not nearly as graceful or colorful!

We then went to look at Indonesian masks in the Ubad Region. We found a little shop on an out-of-the way side street. The craftsman seemed as ancient and wise as the land itself.

I felt a connection to him that was almost scary and had me rethinking reincarnation. His charcoal eyes seemed to illuminate the spirit, although I wasn't sure what that meant to me. I had always wanted that deep abiding faith that would scream out loud in a crowd. I remember going with a girlfriend to see Joel Osteen in Columbia, South Carolina. He is an American preacher and televangelist with the largest Protestant church in the United States. It wasn't my thing, but it was hers, and I was fascinated by how much inspiration she seemed to absorb by watching his telecast on Sundays. So I went with her.

The auditorium was packed to capacity, and even though his sermon seemed to speak in generalities, the audience was mesmerized, and many of the people were raising their hands to the sky, as if receiving some sort of unseen gift. I also wanted what many—the Big Book and members in our 12 step recovery meetings—referred to as being "rocketed into a fourth dimension" due to a spiritual experience. But, maybe since I was an addict, I wanted it *now* instead of *later*. I didn't always want to "pick up those spiritual tools" and actually have to use them on a daily basis, which then in turn, would revolutionize my attitude toward myself, others and life . . . *and toward God*. A part of me still believed I was not worthy of this spiritual experience and God's love. This credence was further fueled by my sexual abuse. I was positive that Ollie had picked me to exploit because not only was I spoiled and marred, but somehow I had deserved it. I had that mystical belief that I would only be transformed if something beyond the mundane occurred. And I was not convinced that this power lay within me and the "we" in the program did not mean someone else would just give it to me. As a result, I instantaneously, at certain times, regressed to child-like thinking and was convinced that some supernatural and astonishing miracle would have to occur for me to be transformed.

So, for that moment, the craftsman had become my Joel Osteen. He introduced himself with a name I could not pronounce or understand. Then he nodded his head with purpose whenever I looked at him and raised his outstretched arms to the sky. When I picked up the masks to examine them, he chanted, "Goodness shouts, evil whispers."

"Whattt?" I asked, staring at his eyes and shuddering involuntarily.

"We have no art. We do everything as well as we can," he said in broken, heavily accented English. I had to bend toward him because not only was he shorter than me, but he was speaking so softly it was as if he was talking an infant to sleep.

"What is it you are trying to get me to understand?" I asked, as if he were sent by God Himself to impart the truth of the universe.

"If you are happy, you can always learn to dance . . ." He smiled crookedly.

I felt like he had joined with my soul and knew more about me than I did myself. Tears welled up in my eyes. Then I noticed Mike chuckling under his breath and motioning for me to go outside.

"Sweetie," he said, as if talking to a wayward child, "he obviously doesn't know much English and is just repeating some well-known Balinese proverbs to impress you. I don't think he is a mystic . . . I think he is trying to manipulate you into buying his masks." Mike had studied the Balinese culture some.

"Oh, I said in a dejected voice, "and I thought I was having one of those spiritual experiences they talk about in the rooms."

Mike laughed so hard I thought his eyes would pop out of his head. It made me laugh. So that's what we did on that side street in Bali—we laughed. Then Mike took my hand in his, and we went back in the shop and purchased two masks. The craftsman beamed at us and said, "Skill is only a rumor until it reaches the muscle."

Toward the end of our trip, I took a Balinese dance class, which proved my theory that I have no poise. I was concentrating so hard at doing it right that my feet rebelled and took off running ahead of me. I fell with a surprised moan that sounded somewhere between a calf being born and someone having a fake orgasm. Both Mike and I laughed so hard at my awkwardness that tears sprung from our eyes like an artesian well, and we were sure the instructor thought all Americans were demented and soulless!

Still, even though our trip was awesome, I was glad to be flying back home. Mike bought first class tickets for our return flight, which was a surprise and made the trip home much more endurable. I couldn't wait to see Satchmo! Debbie was taking care of him. I had skyped Debbie and Satchmo while in Bali just to let Satchmo know I was thinking about him. Debbie thought I was slightly insane, but humored me. I couldn't wait to greet him and roll around on the floor with him when I got home. Mike seemed to look forward to seeing him as well, even though his response was, "I don't even like that dog!"

Before we could get in our front door well, Satchmo pounced on us. Debbie had come and fed, walked, watered him (most of the time he had stayed at her house), and vacated the premises, knowing we would enjoy coming home without having to exchange pleasantries with anyone. She had watered the plants and cleaned the house. It seemed to welcome us home almost as well as Satchmo. Satchmo wagged, danced, bumped and nuzzled us. We both rolled on the floor with him, played tug with his rope and went outside with him to walk the grounds. Afterward, we gave him a treat and collapsed on the couch. Luckily we had asked for the following day off from work, so we didn't have to get up in the wee hours of the morning and start our work routine with jet lag pulling at our brains.

I brought Debbie a wonderfully original painting in Bali that I knew she would like. I felt a wave of gratitude wash over me. Sometimes, I just didn't appreciate all that there was to value and be thankful for in my life. But at this moment, I was fully aware of my many blessings, and whispered thank you to the God of my understanding. I scanned my surroundings and was pleased. Mike had fallen asleep on the couch. Satchmo was half on the floor and half on the couch with his head planted on Mike's chest and was softly snoring. I chuckled to myself, amazed that Satchmo could sleep in that position. *Even the most advanced yoga instructor probably can't do that*, I mused.

* * *

Life got into full swing. But the court case loomed in the near distance like a cat stalking its prey.

I received another one of those life-changing calls late Thursday afternoon.

"Hello. May I speak to Rachel Rheney?" My married name still made my heart skip a beat.

"This is she. How can I help you?" The voice on the other end did not seem familiar, and I felt a wave of uncertainty come over me.

"This is Dr. Rhols, an emergency physician at Mission Hospital. I'm calling about Maija Pevaroff. She has had a massive stroke and is in intensive care. You are listed as her emergency contact. I understand that her husband passed away several years ago and she has no children. Could you please come down to our facility? I'm afraid she is not doing well . . ." She spoke with a voice taking on that tone that funeral directors have when they are trying their best to console you.

"I will be there as quickly as I can," I responded, as I felt a crushing weight descend on my heart. Hurriedly I called Mike and related what was going on. I drove to the hospital with my hands gripping the steering wheel so tightly my knuckles looked white.

I literally trotted inside as the doors automatically opened. I asked in a piercing voice how to get to intensive care. My voice sounded scratchy—as if I smoked too many cigarettes—and it seemed to bounce back at me. I pushed the button to the Intensive Care Unit so the doors would open, and I distractedly washed my hands with the hand sanitizer that was mounted to the wall, as I waited for someone to buzz me in.

A nurse came and took me to the room Maija was in. It had a glass wall looking out on to the nurse's station. She was lying in a hospital bed with all sorts of IVs and machines gathered round her like guests at a burial. My throat felt dry as if I had been lost in the desert for a week. My eyes burned with tears. She was not responsive. I picked up her weathered hand and stroked it.

"Maija, its Rachel. I'm here. You are not alone . . . oh, Maija." The nurse instinctively knew to leave the room once she had attended to her duties. Maija's eyes were open, but I didn't know if she saw me or not. I felt she did on one hand, but on the other, she seemed to be in a distant land. Her face looked softer somehow, and younger, but at the same time, she looked very tired. I talked to her non-stop. I told her how much I loved her and how sorry I was for not having found more time to spend with her. I apologized for everything I knew I had done that was self-centered, thoughtless and just wrong. I talked until my voice was barely audible. And then she died. When she did, a tear escaped from the corner of her eye. And I cried with her.

Several nurses came in and swooped in on her, all business and efficiency. I was almost pushed out of the way. I quickly stepped to the side and backed out of the room just as Mike came in. I fell into his arms and sobbed. He stroked my hair and held me and whispered in a cracked voice, " I've got you, baby . . . I've got you."

I felt something shift inside of me. It was as if my heart was a huge boulder placed precariously on the side of a cliff, shaking with the wind slightly, making strange noises as if it was getting ready to crash but never does. Then, one day, it does fall, but miraculously does not break into a million little pieces as I had thought it would.

Mike and I drove home in silence, at first holding hands while he drove. (Debbie had a friend drop her off at the hospital and picked up my car and drove it home for me.) Mike had burned me a CD with all my favorite "spiritual music." It had everything from Eric Clapton's, "Tears in Heaven," to Dave Matthew's "The Maker." He instinctively turned up the volume for me. And we did what we do that made us whole . . . we sang.

I wrote a poem for Maija that I read at her memorial service:

Another Bright Blue Star

ANOTHER BRIGHT BLUE STAR was a bumper sticker she'd put on my car.
She had an opinion on politics, rearing children, integrity and life—
A clear voice that carried on the rushing wind like a shooting star,
Roots dug deep into the hard-crusted earth as a serrated knife.

Maija reached deeply into the crevices of any scarred heart,
Knowing instinctively when to provide smiling words
Or to profoundly listen, which set her light years apart
Setting the spirit free like a startled flock of boisterous birds.

Marching for Peace with the decisive flair of a drum majorette
Or caring for deprived, lost souls who always asked for more,
She was a woman of unambiguous crystal vision we seldom met,
A strong, hand-hewn oak pedestal on a worn linoleum floor.

A traveler with bags always packed and a mind ready to learn
Reading voraciously with the inquisitiveness of a newborn,
She shared her view without entanglement or words left to burn
Inspiring us to find our own significance without scorn.

Like a shimmering, tender petal that falls from a pale-colored rose,
We will contemplate our loss that brings us to a spiritual stalemate
Questioning a bitter reality and accepting that only God knows
Why "Bad things happen to good people", such is called fate.

So, I look to the night air and stars that gather so bright above,
Remembering her brightness, quiet wit and embracing grace
How she stoked the fire of individuality in those she met with love,
Giving thanks for this gift that was bestowed, but taken in haste.

I will miss you and you'll always have a piece of my heart …
TSA (That Sweet Addict)"

I read as if I were reading to her, with a humble fervor, if there is such a thing. I was oblivious to who was there, and since I still struggled with being a "people pleaser," this was quite a feat. I was mindful of my breath and my heartbeat. I could hear my voice rise and fall with emotion. Afterward, a lot of people who came to pay tribute to Maija walked up to me with tears in their eyes and shared how much my poem had meant to them. I smiled bravely, and thanked them, knowing I probably would not recall their faces the following day. All my nerve endings felt soldered. I buried the poem with her.

I knew this was a stage in the grief process, but I had the sense that everyone I had lost had joined hands and was sitting on my heart, and I was just an observer. And I knew that I would survive and that this feeling would pass if I just allowed myself to be with it and not try and deny my emotions as they came.

Mike and I grew even closer during this time. We had been through a civil war together and a truce had finally been made. I knew that grief sometimes ripped relationships apart, so I attributed what drew us closer to the strength of our spiritual program and willingness to vent our feelings, no matter how jumbled they might be.

"It's as if I am holding a smoldering ember, and when it first starts to burn my skin, I pass it to you to hold for a while . . ." Mike said off the top of his head when we were sharing one morning while lying in bed. *Mike has the heart of a poet*, I thought. *William Blake has nothing on him.*

Mike had a realistic dream about Julia and awakened with tears in his eyes. I didn't care if he had morning breath or beard stubble; I was in awe of how incredibly beautiful he seemed in that moment.

Of course, we were who we were and sometimes could still get in really ridiculous arguments about mundane things. And the grief and stress of the last year seemed to make these arguments even more absurd.

One evening, while sitting in the living room, both of us reading, a thunderstorm raised its head without notice. The winds whipped the trees into a frenzied dance, limbs were breaking and falling to the ground, the lights flickered on and off, and the rain pounded our metal roof, sounding like a hundred African drummers. Neither of us thought to roll down the umbrella on our outdoor furniture, so it took flight and slammed against the side of the house with such force the metal pole bent.

I glared at Mike as if it was his fault (we had just purchased this set).

"Why didn't you roll the umbrella down?" I snapped in an irate voice. I rushed outside in the rain and stared at the broken pots and shards of pottery littered on the deck. I stomped and clomped back into the house with neither grace nor dignity.

"It broke some of my favorite pots of succulents," I stated in an overly melodramatic voice approximating a tone that I would have if a crime against humanity had occurred.

Mike jumped off the couch in the same way I imagined a drunk might react if his pants were on fire after he passed out with a still-lit cigarette.

"Who gives a flying crap? It's just stuff. You act as if I have a direct line to the weather gods! I am so sick of you blaming everything on me. I never do anything right!" And with that last statement, he cleared off the coffee table with one swoop of his arm and sent his coffee cup and other items to the ground.

I stared at him in disbelief. He abruptly left the room, went outside, got in his car and drove off. He didn't come back for over an hour.

I texted him after about forty-five minutes with an amends of sorts, asking him if he wanted to divorce me. He did not respond back. I felt sick, a ball of fear gathering itself in the pit of my stomach. I wailed in the same way I would if my best friend had just been murdered. Satchmo trotted up to me and bumped me. Absently, I stroked his fur and lambasted myself for being so reactive, self-centered and dramatic. I always thoroughly abused myself in my head whenever I lost my composure. I don't think it made things any better, but it was a habit. I was not my own best friend, this was for sure.

When he drove back up the driveway, Satchmo and I were standing at the door. Satchmo's backside was wagging back and forth, but I looked like I had been punched in the stomach, or at least that is what Mike told me later after we had make-up sex and laughed at our antics.

"I don't expect us to be perfect, beautiful. I just expect us to try and be the best we can be, and if we aren't, to own it," Mike said more to himself than to me.

It was agreed that we needed to get back into the habit of reading from one of our meditation books each morning together to start the day with the right focus. Sometimes we would talk about it, sometimes not. But it did seem to help and we were looking for solutions.

* * *

Becca and I were subpoenaed for both trials, as expected. Brian had been charged with the murder of Travis. Randolph B. Walker was charged with the sale and delivery of a Schedule I drug to Julia and second degree murder. Mike was subpoenaed to the latter trial.

After a hearing was held and the judge determined there was enough evidence to proceed to trial, Brian had been incarcerated in the county jail for a year prior to his court date. No one was willing to bail him out. I heard that no one went to visit him the entire time he was incarcerated. The trial was scheduled and postponed several times before it was actually heard.

There was direct evidence in that Brian confessed. He struck a plea bargain between Brain's court-appointed attorney and the criminal prosecutor. In addition to the direct evidence, there was substantial circumstantial evidence to support the facts—Brian had Travis's ring; the investigators found Travis's ring finger, or what was left of it, in

Brian's apartment—so both parties agreed, as well as Brian, for him to be charged with first degree manslaughter. The judge sentenced him to not less than ten years or not more than 29 nine years. Neither Becca nor I were required to testify.

Walker's trial was altogether different. I invited Becca to stay with us during the duration of the trial, as much to support me as to support her. Mike gallantly tried to get more time off of work, but we agreed it would be better if he were put "on-call" because we needed the money. I, too, worked the first part of the trial, but in the end, took some time off on the advice of my coworkers. My mind could not seem to focus on what was right in front of me most days. I agreed that it was probably best if I sat with Becca on those hard wooden benches and provided her some comfort. I would lean forward, listening for the undertones in the judge's voice, straining to pick up any hidden meaning. Both Becca and I tried to decipher the facial expressions on each juror and shared these perceptions with each other day and night. Some sketchy characters sat in the courtroom following the trial. We were more than paranoid. We were hypervigilant and startled easily. It was maddening. We were obsessing about the trial relentlessly, and it was taking its toll on our serenity. I was glad that Debbie and a few others of our support network in the program, including Mike, took notice. Otherwise, both of us might have relapsed ... it's hard to say.

People from the rooms brought 12 Step meetings to our house, and many would come to the trial periodically as a show of support. Groans escaped when anyone thought justice wasn't being served or when comments made by the defense attorney seemed to be in the defendant's favor. The judge cautioned the courtroom with stern admonishments, "If you cannot be quiet during these proceedings, I will gladly have you removed." Then a hush would settle among us like quiet on a riverbank in early morning.

The defense attorney, Jay McCormack, was a balding, obnoxious, obtuse man, from my perspective. Maybe he was doomed from the start because of his position in this theatrical three-ring circus, or maybe he was just loathsome to the core. At times he seemed so insensitive to anyone but his client that I envisioned him the devil incarnate. I knew he was probably being paid an obscene amount of money since Randolph B. Walker, alias "Scramble," the defendant, was just a piece of a larger puzzle. This made him even more horrific.

When I took the stand to testify, McCormack picked apart my language as if I did not know the meanings of words. He assassinated my character, regardless of my recovery or the work I did. He focused primarily on my addiction.

"Ms. Rheney, could you please tell the court about your relationship with the defendant?"

"I, uh, knew him because we ran around in some of the same circles of friends," I answered, knowing that sounded ridiculous since none of the people I associated with then were my friends. They had been just my party buddies.

"What did you do with those so-called friends?" he asked.

I looked at Becca bug-eyed and then down at my lap.

"We partied together," I murmured into my empty hands.

"Can you tell me what 'partied together' means?" McCormack approached the stand.

I looked up defiantly. This was not about my past! This was about some low-life manipulating a young girl who was trying to pull her life together, which ended up killing her!

"We took drugs and drank!" I spat out. I turned imploringly to the judge. "Can I explain, your honor?"

"Just answer the questions. We don't want these proceedings to drag out any longer than necessary," McCormack coldheartedly interjected. The judge never said a word. I had heard that both he and McCormack had zero tolerance for drug addicts and no understanding of addiction. McCormack must have lowered his standards now that he was getting paid by one.

McCormack did the same thing to Becca. During her testimony, the color seemed to drain out of her face like a first tattoo where the colors fade over time and all you see essentially is the outline. I wished I was getting a tattoo just to feel those needles pricking my skin as a distraction from the enormous weight of negative feelings I was experiencing. Shame had a way of slapping me senseless and it stung more than any tattoo needles. McCormack cunningly destroyed any chance we had of being credible witnesses. Only Mike came across looking respectable.

Then there was the media frenzy, which I found unnerving to say the least. I now understood why we sometimes hear about a well-known celebrity who lost control and pummeled some unsuspecting, all-be-it intrusive news reporter. Whatever the stories were, whether written or on the local news station, they seemed to relate just half of what actually happened or was really said. And it seemed to me that the criminals' sad life stories were embellished and emphasized, while the victims' seemed to be forgotten.

I was glad that halfway into the trial my brother Thomas came up to provide support. He was able to shed some light on the judicial system. Did it make me feel any more confident about the proceedings? Probably not. But at least I understood some of the reasoning behind the objections and why they were either overruled or sustained.

While the jury deliberated, we all went out for lunch at a local cafeteria. Nervous tension filled the air. Becca and a couple of others went outside to smoke. Becca had quit for a while, and then took to smoking "vapor" cigarettes. I noticed she pulled a box of Marlboros from her pocketbook. Her eyes looked bloodshot and tired. My heart ached for her.

"This is unbearable," I said out loud, surprised at myself when I heard it bounce off the walls of the waiting room outside the courtroom we had gathered in before leaving.

"Yeah it is," Debbie said. "But we will get through this. What doesn't kill us makes us stronger." She was always there when I needed her most. Another friend from the rooms, Tamara, suggested we join hands and say the Serenity Prayer. We found each other's hands, bowed our heads and said it in unison, not worried about who was looking or listening in. It was comforting.

* * *

It took two, long days for the jury to make its decision. We piled into the courtroom to await the verdict. When they announced, "Not Guilty," we all gasped out loud at once, and it seemed to suck the oxygen out of the room. Everyone was crying, or muttering or looking down in utter disbelief.

Randolph B. Walker got up and gave his attorney a bear hug, looked at the back of the courtroom at some unsavory characters and grinned. They got up all at once and left. The bailiff, who had been standing off in an obscure corner of the courtroom, sprang to life with the same zest I imagined a young girl at her first party would have when asked to dance. *He takes his role seriously*, I supposed, with a scratch of bitterness directed at all entities resembling authority. He was an officer of the court, and it was his responsibility to maintain peace. When Walker's compadres abruptly left the courtroom, it was if that was permission for everyone to move around at once and start commenting on the verdict. So the bailiff admonished the court. "Be still and quiet in order that the judge can give his parting remarks, or I will be glad to escort you out.

During this little spiel, the judge earned back a little of my respect. Looking down from the bench, the judge said, as he removed his glasses and laid them purposely on the polished surface, "Mr. Walker, you have been gifted by luck and nothing else. It is my belief that you are most likely guilty of the crime you were charged with, but, as instructed by me at the beginning of these proceedings, the jury was not able to prove beyond a 'reasonable doubt' your guilt. If this were a civil case, it is my opinion that the preponderance of the evidence was adequate enough to have found you guilty, as it requires a lower standard of proof. However, this is a criminal case. The evidence presented was mostly circumstantial and the burden of proof was not clear and convincing. As a result, you were found not guilty and are free to go."

The judge paused, cleared his throat, fiddled with his glasses for a moment and then looked head-on at Walker and said, enunciating every word, "However, I would advise you to leave our gracious state and not come back. I do not want to see your face ever again in my courtroom. I would fully support our dedicated law enforcement officers to arrest you if they even *think* you have broken a law before you leave. In fact, I would applaud them for arresting you on the spot with hopes that I would be able to preside at your hearing once again, because I don't believe you would be so lucky a second time."

I felt vindicated, and for this I was grateful. And knowing that Brian had been convicted of first-degree manslaughter in the murder of Travis made me feel like some justice prevailed. Still, when I looked at both Becca and Mike, it was not gratitude I saw. When Becca stomped down the courtroom stairs, she dramatically took a swipe at the American flag that was flanking them and knocked it crashing to the floor. Luckily, no one else was around when she did. I did not know how to fix any of this, so I retreated into myself as I had done so many times in the past. But for some reason, I heard the words: "Be still and know that I am . . ." flutter in my head like a butterfly grazing a wildflower. My spiritual awakening they talked about in the 12 Step rooms lifted its head off the pillow, and it was comforting. I cried silent tears.

Mike and I each relied on our spiritual program to help us through the next several days. Life returned to its usual hum, and we could not afford to let our grief and anger immobilize us. We reached out as much as we could to Becca and encouraged her to stay in constant contact with her sponsor and support network.

I cannot say I was totally surprised when I got the call from Becca several weeks later. The alarm clock glared that it was two in the morning. Becca slurred her words as she practically shouted into the phone, "I can't do this . . . I'm so fucking tired . . ." I knew better than to do a 12 Step call by myself, and I knew instinctively it would be better if I brought another female as opposed to a male, even though Mike was more readily accessible. So I called Debbie after I got reassurance from Becca that she was not going to harm herself.

"Hello . . . ?" Debbie sleepily said into the phone.

"Uh . . . we have a problem. Becca's loaded," I said, "and she needs us. I don't know how long she's been using, 'cause I've been busy back at work, but she's in trouble."

"Well, then give me a moment or two to pull myself together, and I'll come by and get you."

Mike was leaning on his arms, eyes open. "Can I do anything, baby?"

I assured him that Debbie and I had it under control. "We got this. Don't worry, Poppabear. You have a long day ahead of you, and I know you need your beauty rest." I kissed him lightly on the head, rubbed his shoulders and got out of bed.

Mike was admitting two teenagers into the inpatient facility the following day. He looked relieved when I said it.

Debbie and I went to Becca's house. We knocked hard on the door several times. When she yelled out for us to come in, we did. She was sprawled out on the couch, half on and half off. She looked and smelled horrible. I thought to myself that I probably looked very similar when Debbie found me.

Becca was moaning, cussing and crying all at once. For some reason, Debbie and I fumbled around with words to say. We both squished together with Becca on the couch.

"Becca, you know the deal," Debbie finally said in a monotone, as if she had been emptied of all compassion. I looked at her. Debbie looked exhausted. I had always thought of her as an endless supply of serenity and hope. I guess I forgot she was human and was an alcoholic addict as well. I wondered for a second if her recovery was in jeopardy, but dismissed it.

"Oh, screw you, Debbie. You are so perfect. Who gives a flying fuck? I don't care about you or anyone. What the hell are you looking at, Rachel?" Becca screeched, fueled by some inner rage that I hadn't seen this closely before. Of course, I had never been around her when she was loaded and I wasn't.

"We are trying to save your life, Becca," I said with tears in my eyes. "You know in your heart of hearts that this isn't going to make the pain go away. We'll help you get into a detox center if need be. Whatever it takes, we will be there with you. I hope you know that."

Absentmindedly, I began to eat by huge handfuls the stale mixed nuts she had in a bowl on her coffee table. I became so absorbed in cramming them into my mouth that I just plain stopped listening to anything Becca and Debbie were saying.

"Rachel!" Debbie barked. "What do you think?" It became clear that Becca was resistant to anything we were saying or doing.

"I don't know ... you're my sponsor ... why are you asking me?" I implored with color rising to my face. I knew that I was trying to avoid feeling anything and did not want to be there.

"Well, you are a social worker!" she snapped back as she repositioned herself on the couch.

Becca had passed out and was snoring loudly.

"I guess we could leave her a note on the table and call her in the morning to check on her," I answered reluctantly. "I don't think she is going anywhere. Maybe we could have the police do a health and safety check?"

I called Becca the next morning, but she told me "quit harassing me." I then called Debbie, who was rather curt as well. I felt dejected. I admonished myself and told myself it wasn't about me. But, it felt like it *was* somehow. I shared what I was willing to share at my meetings ... and with Mike.

"You gotta let it go, baby. Quit obsessing about it," Mike said glibly.

"So, how do you propose I do that, Mr. 12 Step program?" I knew as soon as I said it that it was the wrong thing to say.

"You are going to quit snapping at me! Everything is not my fault!" he threw back at me.

"Oh, fuck you!" I reacted with my usual response whenever I felt emotionally spent and did not know how to get to the core of my feelings, feel them and move on.

It was as if we were in one of those freak highway accidents where one car kept rear ending the one in front of it until there was a twenty-two car pile-up.

I banged out and jumped into my car. It was early evening. The moon was full and seemed to illuminate my bottled and capped up anger, which exploded with the same force a can of soda does when shaken up and then opened. I cried—no, wailed—with snot shooting out my nose like lava from a volcano. Then I started to curse even though this had been one of my "character defects" I had vowed to correct. No matter how much emphasis I placed on it, "Oh fudge" just didn't seem to provide the same degree of release as some of my favorite expletives did. My car appeared to operate on autopilot and drove me to the mall where in probably five minutes tops, I consumed three peanut butter cookies and a mocha frappe at the little coffee shop located at its center. Then I went to the beauty salon and got my hair trimmed and highlights put in. I topped it off with a whirlwind of spending. I bought items I didn't really need. Ah, such a predictable pattern of emotion-dodging. Sugar, caffeine, vanity and shopping. Well, those things never led me off in handcuffs, I rationalized. I was angry at this disease. It destroyed lives. I didn't understand it. It really was "cunning, baffling and powerful," as they drone on in meetings. I was mad at everyone and everything. And I was enjoying my anger for a minute or two. Eventually, I started to laugh and pray and I think, even burp somewhere in there. It was how I "let go."

* * *

Later that week, Debbie called me and apologized.

"I got my own stuff, Rachel. This whole thing has been draining. It is hard as hell to watch those we care about destroy themselves. I get mad at this disease too. And sometimes, not meaning to, I can get judgmental. Maybe it's because I don't tolerate that kind of behavior from me," she shared, "and believe me, before I got clean and sober, I acted in some of the same ways." I had never heard this admission before. Probably because I was always focused on me when I talked to her.

"Oh, I guess even Wonder Woman has to crash sometimes," I joked. "I hope I never gave the impression I expected you to be perfect. I only expect that from me."

"Well, I guess you are my sidekick, Robin—no that's Batman's, not Wonder Woman's!" she said laughing.

"So, have you heard from Becca? No one has seen her at any meetings. She doesn't answer the phone when I call. I text her periodically just to let her know she is in my thoughts and prayers. I guess that's all I can do," I said almost to myself.

"No, I haven't. What they always say: 'We didn't cause it, can't cure it and can't control it,'" Debbie reminded.

"I know, I know." Sometimes I hated hearing those same lines being said over and over even if they were true. I said my goodbyes and hung up. I looked down. Satchmo was sitting at my feet, his nubby tail thumping on the hardwood floor. For a minute, I wondered if Satchmo had a "phantom" long tail similar to someone who had lost a limb but still perceived sensations in the location of the lost limb. I shook my head free of my random thought, chuckling at its absurdity and looked at Satchmo who continued to thump.

"Wanna go outside? Gotta pee?" He got up and did his backward dance toward the front door. I know that a lot of people think dogs don't go to heaven and that God resides in only people, but I am certain that my Higher Power radiated from the soft brown eyes of a puppy, especially mine.

* * *

I ran into Becca in odd places but never at a meeting. The last time I saw her was at the library. Apparently, she had come up with a scam hitting up patrons with a story of victimization complete with the tears. She would tell them she had an abusive partner and was trying to get away from him. She was panhandling. She looked spent. Becca had no car and was homeless. Unfortunately she had lost her home in a tornado of addiction. She was not only drinking, but had become sucked into using opiates on a daily basis. Prescription opiates had become a huge problem in Asheville. It seemed when the "war on drugs" eliminated one substance, another one popped up. Crack had been the main problem at one time. Now it was prescription opiates. As soon as the physicians who prescribed these started taking stock of the damage created and quit prescribing them so frequently, heroin started regaining its popularity.

I did my best to convince Becca to stop trying to kill herself. She seemed oblivious to anything I had to say and had a one-track mind. "I need to see a friend of mine," she repeated over and over, making no pretense of listening to me. I drove her to one of the housing projects and dropped her off as she directed. I gave her a few bucks, knowing full well she would not use the money to eat, but to score. She turned to me and said, "I will pull you down before you pull me up." I cried all the way home. Later I heard she had been walking down the highway stoned out of her mind and got hit by a car and killed.

It wasn't long after that I found myself at a bar. I had been driving home from a work-required educational seminar when my car pulled into a seedy roadside tavern. The gravel crunched under my tires as I parked next to a couple of trucks. On one side of this establishment there was a line of Harley Davidson motorcycles. A young couple pushed against the plaster walls so hard that I am sure its nondescript design was pressed into the young woman's backside. They were grinding and groping, and he had his oily hand down her pants. I was surprised at my power of observation. I stared for a long time and then got out of my car. When I opened the thick door, I was assaulted by the sweet aroma of marijuana and cigarettes. If it was against the law to smoke in a public place, the patrons obviously didn't give a damn. I smiled. *My kind of place*, I thought.

I adjusted my eyes to the dim lights and scanned the room. Old linoleum covered a floor with the scuffs and scrapes of years of neglect and traffic. It looked like a tribute to the seventies. Aluminum bar stools with red, cracked, plastic covers sat at the bars like Congregationalists waiting for communion. There were two pool tables with small tables and chairs arranged haphazardly around them. A mirror behind the bar looked as if it had not been cleaned since the seventies. However, the bar counter was a thing of beauty. Some crazy-talented craftsman had made it out of a tree trunk and used layers of polyurethane to permanently put in place beer bottle tops from all over the world. It was a testimony to breweries everywhere, but probably did not receive the accolades it deserved in this particular den of iniquity.

  I situated myself at the bar and asked for a shot of Jack Daniels straight. The bartender, a chunky female with a hard stare like the shards of ice in the glass I was about to drink, brought it to me. Her nails were fake, long and painted neon pink and she had rings—made of silver with turquoise and coral stones—on most of her fingers. They were beautiful, ornate designs. On her knuckles was a tattoo: KISS OFF! I liked her immediately. Her deep brown eyes—framed by artfully arched painted eyebrows and deep violet eye shadow—sized me up in an instant, and she seemed to warm up to me immediately as well. Her eyes melted into liquid kindness.

  "You ain't been here before, but you've been to plenty of places like this I think," she said with an observant, knowing gaze.

  I nodded as I stared fixedly at my glass and the brown amber liquid that wanted to pull me into its watery promise of annihilation. She quickly departed as someone from the end of the bar hollered for her attention.

  My mind started its familiar rantings as if several instruments in a band were all being tuned up at once.

  The drums couldn't keep their rhythm, but were always the loudest. The beat was heavy and pulsed with alarming urgency, "Come on now. It's just going to be this one time. No one will know.

You've been through the ringer, and you deserve to forget." Then, if I listened closely, I could make out the faint chords of a piano. I strained to hear the music, and the singer who carried its euphonious melody in words I needed to believe. This voice reminded me of who I was and of the disease that wanted to kill me. I prayed out loud as tears parachuted from my eyes.

The waitress reappeared as quickly as she had departed and said, "I am a friend of a friend of Bill W and I don't think you want this." When I looked up, she winked and her smile was the most beautiful, illuminating smile I believe I had ever seen. No other words were spoken. I got up and tried to slide some money toward her when she covered my hand and pushed it back toward me. Then I walked outside with several cat calls following me from men inside the walls trying to convince me to stay. A flock of birds lifted off the branches in synchronicity on what looked like the only tree for quite a distance. I knew instinctively that my Higher Power had intervened. Bill W is one of the founding fathers of the 12 Step program of Alcoholics Anonymous.

And so it was with addiction. I can never completely understand why one person gets clean and sober and another doesn't. Yes, I understand there are things we have to do. But it never seems as clear and simple as suggested. The only thing I can attribute it to really is God's grace. If I think on it too long, I start getting angry with God. I've seen too many people die from this disease, and I am not sure how God picks and chooses. But then, I suppose, that is where faith comes in. I have to have faith that God really does know what He (or She) is doing. And that's where my problem begins. I guess I don't always have *that* kind of faith on any given day. I have a taste of it sometimes out of the clear blue. And then the more I try to hold onto it, the more it disappears out of my grasp like trying to hold onto ice cream.

Still, my blessings were many. Work was going pretty well, but I had decided I wanted to work with adults with addiction problems. I knew I still struggled with my past history of sexual abuse and that, despite the progress I had made in recovery, it was getting in the way of my being as effective as I could be with the young girls I worked with. I will not deny that I had played a solid part in a few of their roads toward healing, but felt that I might have even interrupted some of their healing process as well. And the culmination of the last year prompted me to do something different. It's not like substance abuse counselors were paid more. Plus I would have to take a state exam. I had already been getting the required supervision. I talked to Mike about it.

"I just want you to be happy. You are so much easier to get along with when you're happy, and you know what they say, 'Happy wife, happy life.' Besides, we have a lot of investments. I have a substantial retirement set aside. Joanne and I split my parents' estate and it was no chump change. I didn't tell you that because I wanted to make sure you loved me for Me," he said with a laugh. "We are not millionaires, but we are comfortable."

So I studied and took the exam and passed, even though I was convinced I wouldn't. I hated tests. When I stood at the window of the exam room and awaited the results, I didn't know if I passed or failed. After the examiner graded it and toyed with me about my results, I thought I would keel over right then and there. The examiner was encapsulated in a glassed booth. I had to stand on tip-toes to see all the way in. He asked me with a blank, unyielding face, "So, do you want to know the results now?" which I construed as bad news. Then, he said with a bright smile, "It looks like you are now a licensed certified addictions counselor!" It turned out I passed with a good margin. I didn't feel brilliant, just relieved.

* * *

I looked in the local newspaper for employment. This was an independent newspaper that provided extensive coverage of local politics, as well as an immeasurable arts and entertainment section, which I pored over to help plan Mike and my extracurricular activities. A lot of human service positions were listed. I applied for one I thought was working with sexual abuse victims and addiction. It turned out to be with male perpetrators just getting out of the prison system. I didn't know that when I went in for the interview. The piece in the classified section just wasn't that clear.

"You'd be facilitating groups and hooking these men up to services to enable them to more easily re-enter society," the woman who was interviewing me declared.

I cut her off abruptly as I felt blood rush to my head. "Oh... I thought this job was working with the victims, not the perpetrators. I don't think this is the job for me due to my history and unresolved anger... I am so sorry I wasted your time." An old familiar anger pulsed through my veins. "Your ad wasn't that specific," I said in a rushed tone. I wanted to run out of there before I just started randomly cursing. This was an emotion I just seemed to have difficulty letting go of. The best I could do was keep it in restraints, shackled and handcuffed like a prisoner of war.

* * *

I finally took a job employed on an ACT (Assertive Community Treatment) team, working with the severely and persistently mentally ill as the substance abuse specialist. An ACT team was an evidence-based practice designed to provide treatment, rehabilitation and support services to the severely and persistently mentally ill whose needs supposedly had not be met by more traditional mental health services. This is an intensive and highly integrated approach based around the concept that people receive better care when their providers work together and meet them where they are, whether it be on the streets, at home or in a family care facility. And if I ever had any doubts about my blessings, this job thoroughly smashed every one of them. The individuals I worked with had to step over and around every socio-economic barrier that existed.

I bumped heads with our social policy and its ever-increasing mound of paperwork put in place to ensure accountability. There was a shortage of funding and adequate resources. It appeared that most of the personnel who had the necessary training and education were put in more administrative positions or had less hands-on interactions with the folks they assisted. These same personnel were buried under a land-fill of forms and many had the gnawed-on cuticles to prove it. In the end, this red tape undermined the quality of services we provided because many of us spent more time staring at the computer than working with the individuals we served. I was always working overtime trying to get this endless work done to guarantee Medicaid approved hours for us to work with our consumers as the State preferred we call them. Medicaid funded what was down on paper, not whether or not the person needed services. On occasion, a client would actually lose services if a mistake had been made on the paperwork submitted, and because of the caseloads and unreasonable timelines for completing the paperwork, many a mistake was made.

This whole process did not allow for much of a person-centered approach. Still, I tried my best to deliver such an approach at my own expense. It meant giving of my time and energy when I was not sure I had the time and energy to give.

Debbie, who was always direct, lectured me about boundaries. I just felt so responsible. I knew how I felt when the array of human service workers I had encountered as a child forgot my story and looked at me, but did not see me because they were inundated with paperwork and just trying to keep up with all the demands their job heaped on them. Of course at that time, I did not have any compassion for my workers because I felt they had no compassion for me. I did not understand their challenges and constraints, nor did I care. I wanted to be validated and not just one of the many who was there demanding help in a system with little resources. And then, because of deinstitutionalization, most human service professionals worked with individuals having chronic and severe mental illness, who were in group homes staffed by a high school-educated workforce being paid minimum wage. And this was usually a 6:1 ratio of residents to staff, allowing little room for these employees to implement any creative or preventive measures while working with their consumers. This staff was frequently too busy or weary addressing emergencies and trying to reduce anxieties generated by a faulty system while serving persons with complex challenges.

At ACT I remember working overtime and being called by direct service staff to one of these group homes at three a.m. the morning. My eyes felt the sting of too little sleep, and I felt disoriented. But I went because it was my job. My client, a young teenage girl, with dyed hair of blue and yellow, was making threats toward her roommate and staff. The staff, not much older than the girl, had not been able to de-escalate the situation, and when I arrived, not only was the client irate, the staff was bordering on coming unhinged as well. It is never a good idea to raise your voice when dealing with clients. And I commiserated with my client. She was sharing a room with a schizophrenic, older women who talked to herself and to her hallucinations, some nights more than others. Much as I tried to get the group home staff not to put these two in a room together, they did. My client suffered from a borderline personality disorder and Post Traumatic Stress Disorder due to severe abuse and neglect when she was a child. She would benefit from being in a room by herself. The situation was bound to become problematic, and I told them so. Still, here I was walking my client around the block, encouraging her to breathe and use her emotional regulation skills, and then essentially tucking her into bed. The older woman, who was not my client, had been given a PRN medication to help her sleep but she had not been receiving it. I had the staff look at her records and administer medication already prescribed. If the group home staff had been better trained and funding had made provisions for single rooms, this incident probably would have been prevented.

After many a day at the office, I usually went straight home, exhausted, turned on the news and heard some heart-wrenching story about how someone with a mental health diagnosis had killed a room full of people and then shot himself or herself. Invariably, this bewildered soul had received deficient mental health services. This further stimulated my internal exasperation with the Medicaid system and North Carolina's judgment of what and how much funding should be allocated to the mental health system.

I often wondered if someone had not reached out to me, and my circumstances had been different, would I have been one of those tortured souls? Would I have been shuffled off to some rundown group home with inadequate funding? I envisioned myself in mismatched clothing, loaded down with psychotropic drugs and repeating inane broken conversational snippets, my eyes looking like someone pried them open with a pair of pliers and they got stuck that way. Sometimes, we look right through such folks as if they don't exist or are rabid animals. They are invisible. Or all we see is what they are *not* instead of what they *could be*. We don't see their potential. I was glad that someone saw what I could be.

The beauty of an ACT team is that we go to where the people live, work, play and unravel. We also get to see their potential as we provide services where they live instead of having them come to an office. Many of the people we would serve simply can't afford gas to come to the therapist's office, don't have a car, or in many cases, don't have a driver's license. People feel more relaxed in their home, or where they live, even if it is on the streets. It is familiar. Also, specific skills, such as parenting or even anger management, can be better demonstrated where the person lives as we get to observe commonplace interactions or obstacles the person faces. Sometimes, that can be a real eye-opener. My first month on the job, I went to visit a gentleman client in the housing projects. He knew ahead of time we had an appointment. I tried to call to remind him, but his phone was out of minutes.

I rode the elevator to the third floor of his building in the heart of downtown Asheville. The chrome doors opened with a squeak. The entire building smelled of disinfectant and spoiled food. In addition, there was a rancid odor like something had died. Cigarette and marijuana smoke lingered in the cold air like steam rising from a manhole cover in New York City. My eyes darted instinctively from side to side as I stepped out onto the worn linoleum that looked so much like others I had seen when visiting clients.

I knocked on the door. I heard muffled voices and other obscure sounds.

"Whatchu want?" A loud, but garbled voice declared.

I identified myself by sliding my card under the door as not to violate any HIPAA regulations. "Leo, it's me. Remember, we had an appointment." I spoke to this solid surface as if it were a live human being.

Leo opened the door. He was scruffy and reeked of body odor and booze. I could see some people stirring around in the background and a couple of empty Mad Dog 20/20 bottles lining the dirty windowsill.

"Ms. Rachel... this ain't a good time," he said. "The Po Po been called. There was a stabbing in the crib next door. Youse need to go." His breathing was loud and made gurgling noises. He seemed to be hyperventilating. He started to close the door in my face. He did not seem to want me to reply.

"You okay? Do I need to hang around?" I asked as I blocked the door. I was trying to sound comforting but had a feeling I was not coming across that way. I was feeling a little panicky myself.

"I'm okay, I promise. But this ain't a good time, like I said. Do youse feel me? "

"I'll call you later and check on you," I said as if that would fix everything. I walked briskly down the hall.

Leo had schizoid affective disorder. He also was an alcoholic. I always knew when he had been drinking because he would smoke incessantly. A man in his early fifties, he had COPD and was a veteran. His hair was like steel wool, and he never picked it out. His head always was adorned by particles of food and lint. Half of his teeth were rotten. He was tall and gangly and had oversized hands and feet. But, there was a gentle side to him and a quick wit. Even though he did not trust me completely, I thought he trusted me as much as he would trust anyone. I found him endearing. And I admired his ability to survive whatever life dealt him. And he had been dealt more than his fair share of bad hands.

I did as I promised and called him later in the day. He sounded non-committal, and I had a hard time scheduling another appointment. Finally, we agreed for me to pick him up in front of his apartment building the following day and take him to the VA office for a scheduled doctor appointment. It would mean allocating half of the day to him because it took a while to navigate the VA system, and then we would have to stop at the store to get groceries en route back to his apartment. I did set a limit on the amount of time spent at the grocery store and encouraged him to make a list of items needed within his budget. During all this, we would have our talk about healthy boundaries and his choice of companions. I was not unrealistic, as I understood 75% of the people in his apartment had "issues" and might not make ideal companions. But he tended to break the rules of his subsidized housing contract and took people he knew off the street and allowed them to reside in his apartment.

I picked Leo up, but had to retrieve him from his apartment. I reminded him that we had arranged to meet in front, but he shrugged and mumbled something about his watch not keeping "good time." And then he smiled, as if it would excuse any and everything. And I succumbed to his hard-to-define charms. Most of my clients were broken and had been cast aside, or in most cases, kicked to the side. Sometimes the best I could do was to accept them as they were and let them know someone genuinely cared about them and believed that the quality of their lives could be improved.

Leo had written his grocery list on an old brown paper bag, which was crumpled up in the inside pocket of his army coat. His coat smelled of age, cigarettes and body odor. I had encouraged him to wash it on occasion, but gave up as he had attributed mystical powers to his coat and thought laundering it would destroy those powers. And who was I to argue? I did try to convince him his powers resided within, but he would just look at me and nod his head as if I were a child.

The VA hospital is enormous. Leo knew where to go and what to do with no problem. Of course, his primary care physician always commented on Leo's lifestyle and need for change, but was resigned to the fact that Leo would change when Leo was ready to change. He discussed his meds and made some adjustments. We brought the list of psychotropic medications and put our heads together to make sure Leo understood his regimen. Of course, we filled Leo's med box on a weekly basis and even then he had a hard time staying on track. When Leo was off his meds, he was not able to deal with the world or his inner monsters at all. At least with an ACT team and considerable monitoring, he was able to function. Maybe not too well by others' standards, but compared to how he functioned off his meds and without services, he was like the difference between Mahatma Gandhi and Attila the Hun.

"So when are youse going to go on a date with me?" he said out of the clear blue while the doctor updated his records on the computer. "I know you like those Puerto Ricans, but I could make you change your mind!"

The doctor looked at me and I looked back at him with a half-smile.

"Now, Leo, you know I am on your ACT team and that would not be professional. We are not allowed to date our clients," I said, not addressing the comment about Puerto Ricans.

"I won't tell anyone," he said and winked. Then he changed subjects completely without taking a breath. "I need some milk. I think it's on my list." He fumbled with his list that was crammed in his pocket. When he pulled it out, some old grimy pennies, some kind of half-sucked-on candy that wasn't in its wrapper and a cigarette butt came out with it. He did not stoop to pick them up.

"Leo, you dropped something," I said. "Why don't you pick that stuff up and get rid of what you don't need?"

He appeared to be responding to inner stimuli and was muttering under his breath, so I repeated myself. He looked at me and then at the floor. He picked up the pennies and shoved them back in his pocket. He threw the candy in the wastepaper basket by the doctor's desk. And then he carefully straightened out the cigarette butt and said in a louder than necessary voice, "I could smoke this later, don't cha know?" For the second time in a few minutes, the doctor and I looked at each other.

"And yeah, I know smoking is going to kill me," he remarked with a defiant stare daring us to say something, "but we all gotta die from something, don't we, doc?"

At the grocery store, Leo tried his best to get an endorsement for him to purchase a bottle of wine. I reminded him of why I was there and how alcohol undermines what his meds were trying to do. Then I emphasized that not only was he an alcoholic who suffered from liver disease, but unceremoniously went into detail of the last time he had "given in" and what had occurred. Leo insisted on buying several gallons of milk even though I tried to educate him on the expiration date and the milk turning sour before he could drink it all. But Leo refused to listen and piled five gallons of milk into his cart. I never did understand his reasoning or lack thereof. I took him back to his meager apartment, helped him unpack his groceries, filled his pillbox with a stern reminder for him to take his medication and went home.

The authorities found Leo by the side of the road a few days later, unconscious. He had been beaten up, and someone had stolen his most prized possession, a pocket watch that had been handed down from his grandfather. Although he did not pay particular attention to his hygiene even on a good day, he always kept his pocket watch wound and polished. Leo was sicker than sick, both physically and mentally, when they found him; he required hospitalization. The hospital discharge social worker and I managed to get Leo placement with the Asheville Buncombe Community

Christian Ministry (ABCCM) Veterans Restoration Quarters (VRQ) since he had lost his housing. VRQ supplied homeless veterans with transitional housing and a huge array of other useful services.

"Leo, you almost got yourself killed. What is it going to take for you to do something different?" I asked, looking at him inquisitively but with obvious compassion.

"Oh, I hope this is it. I am a worn-out black man," he said as he looked down at his feet. "And I do appreciate youse, Ms. Rachel. Youse always tell me like it is. I need that you know. You think you could buy me a pack of smokes?"

Instead, we settled on a bag of Reese's Pieces and made arrangements for him to go to a 12 step education meeting that night at the VA hospital. Early on, he only sporadically attended this group that the facilitators offered to take the "mystery" out of a 12 step program so a newcomer would know what to expect should he go. But, for whatever reason, he began to attend more often and eventually transitioned to the VA's 12 step processing group for veterans. Leo finally allowed himself to open up to the support these groups offered and found a kinship there that I could not give him.

"These are my peoples, Ms. Rachel. I might even be able to help some of them like youse been helping me," he said with a flash in his eyes. I blushed and beamed at the same time. I couldn't be any prouder of him than if he were my own family. I knew he had essentially done all the hard work, I had just been driving him around so he could do it. VRQ took over as primary case manager, and Leo began to entrench himself in other programs that the VA offered. ACT eventually closed Leo's case. He was doing too well for our services.

I worked with many Leos. They were all different, but all the same. Their everyday clashes and melees would probably have made the Pope crumble if he had encountered them. Sometimes, my best just didn't seem good enough. There were not many huge successes like Leo. Success was measured in much smaller increments. Sometimes all I did was listen. Being heard was something many of these folks never experienced. Delusions and paranoia can create rifts and fear. I did not fear them. I was fearful *for them* at times. Many lived in squalor or demeaning situations. *Together* we would explore and implement ways to make their lives better and more manageable. As a result, I worked the same long hours as I had in my previous job. And so it went. But I loved the work, maybe not the paperwork, but I loved my clients and the team I worked with.

As long as I got my work done, our agency was supportive of my creative process. I attended art therapy workshops and honed up on my skills working with persons with dual diagnoses. I got my compulsory certification in Dialectical Behavior Therapy (DBT) and motivational interviewing so I could legitimately use it in my work. DBT is a cognitive-behavior-based approach that emphasizes the biopsychosocial facets of treatment, suggesting that some people have a more intense response to life situations and need to learn habitual coping skills to manage these extreme emotional upheavals. Motivational interviewing was developed initially to work with problem drinkers and resolve their potential ambivalence toward treatment. It is very individual-centered, goal-oriented and focused, as opposed to the client lying supine on a couch and exhaustingly exploring and rehashing why one became who one became as I speculated some Freudian theorist might expect. During the course work required to get these certifications, I most always found tools that I could apply in my own life. I remember more than once people I crashed into while getting high chastising me for being "too intense" and questioning why I couldn't just relax and "enjoy the high." Instead, while intoxicated, I many times entered into sobering discussions, which, depending on who they were with, escalated into a shouting match or sometimes a physical altercation.

I distantly remember one such confrontation happening at a bar I had been frequenting back before I met Mike. This particular occurrence was with a man who declared himself a "disabled vet." During the course of our dialogue, I made an unmindful remark: "All pain is relative." I suppose it was in reference to war. I do not remember the in-between parts of this conversation. I do remember somehow linking my sexual abuse and rape into this narrative I had embarked upon. Then, I recall him saying something like, "You must have deserved it," and me coming undone. He was huge and muscular. I am not sure what his disability was. I exploded on him anyway. My hands and feet were chopping and slicing the earth as I tried to hit him. Some biker-type characters picked me up and carried me out of there, reprimanding me all along, saying, "He will tear you from limb to limb. He doesn't care if you are a *girl*," which seemed to reignite my rage. They ended up dumping me unceremoniously somewhere. I must have managed to get home as that is all I can recall.

So, the core mindfulness skills emphasized in DBT seemed fitting to help me "regulate my emotions" as the experts kept harping on. I found it less offensive to my sensibilities and convinced myself that I was just more *passionate* about life than the average person, which is why I felt so *intensely* (whether under the influence or not). It did give me a more thorough understanding of the people I supported. As a result, I appreciated my job more. I felt I had purpose and that I was in my element. I was exhausted most days, but satisfied.

* * *

Mike was working just as hard as I was so we seemed to bump into each other only on weekends. But we filled the weekends with projects, entertaining friends and family, and living. We played our guitars. Mike knew someone who tuned my upright piano, and I was playing again. We were taking a carpentry class together. Both of us were so busy we did not notice that we were letting our recovery program slide. We seemed to think working in the field would suffice and make up for our lack of a spiritual focus. We were attending meetings only sporadically. I stopped calling Debbie as often. I think Mike fired his sponsor and never got another. The more we stopped going to meetings, the more we stopped going to meetings.

Mike seemed to have become obsessed with my shortcomings overnight. And according to him, I was not pleased with anything he said or did. Little comments became huge slaps in the face. It would either fuel an out-of-control battle of the wills, or we both seemed to simper away in distress.

One weekend afternoon, Mike was watching the Cowboys play football on television. I knew more about football than he seemed to give me credit for. Both my father and mother were avid football fans. And Thomas not only played football in high school, he also played fantasy football every chance he could. I just didn't like the Cowboys. Not for any concrete reason. Probably for some obscure reason having to do with their cheerleaders—their miniscule, revealing uniforms and my belief that somehow that was demeaning to women and that was the team's fault. I didn't remember Mike watching as much football before we got married. So my mind conjured up the thought that he was doing so because he wanted to pant over the cheerleaders. It never occurred to me that the cheerleaders really didn't get much television-viewing time and that Mike was enjoying watching the team winning season. This erroneous thought was an old disturbing pattern from my past when I was convinced that all men were lechers at heart. And lately I seemed to pick up resentments like empty cans on the highway.

In an attempt to be a "part of" his experience and ignore what my mind was telling me, I asked, "Who are the Cowboys playing?" But my voice was forced. When Mike didn't answer, I looked at the screen and saw they were playing Arizona.

"Well, since I really don't know much about Arizona, I guess I'll pull for the Cowboys," I remarked.

Mike erupted. "You could care less about the Cowboys! You can watch something else!" he retorted while turning the channel to HGTV, which I knew he didn't really care for.

"Damn it, Mike, why do you always assume I am trying to manipulate you?" I snapped back while picking up the remote and making a big deal about turning the station back to the football game. "I like football more when I pick a side. I was just making a remark out loud in an effort to show some interest in what *you* are interested in!"

We got into a little tug-of-war with the remote. Finally we both gave up while he sat stone-faced watching the game and I huffed off and found something else to do.

We both apologized later on, but not with the same fervor and ardent lovemaking we had in the past. Of course, then I started obsessing about that and was convinced our marriage was on the skids. Wisely, I didn't share these negative thoughts with Mike or it might have been the beginning of the end for all I know. I did remember what the Big Book said about making unreasonable demands and wanting more than our share of attention. I remembered, but I still did not go to a meeting, which my sponsor always suggested I do when "uncomfortable in my skin."

I started to take things personally more and more. I began to have my usual array of nightmares, which for a while, had stopped. It was always about being violated in some way or another, trying to get away, and whoever it was that was violating me, laughing the entire time as they performed great atrocities on my person.

Mike began to eat more, watch more television and exercise less.

I knew better than to make snide remarks, but sometimes my mouth bolted ahead of my head to get to home plate and I just let it slide out.

"Turning into a couch potato aren't you?" I said as I glared at him laid up on the couch with remote and snacks less than an arm's reach away.

"So what!" he volleyed without even looking my way. I rolled my eyes, picked up the car keys and with a lot of excess noise, got Satchmo and declared we were going for a hike.

The next day was a workday. In the small spiral notebook that we wrote messages to one another on, I drew him a little picture of a monkey indicating:

> I LOVE YOU, I LOVE YOU, I LOVE YOU I DO,
> BUT DON'T GET EXCITED, I LOVE MONKEYS TOO.

An accompanying message professed my undying love and asked for forgiveness That afternoon, I got a message from one of his coworkers requesting that I call her back right away.

"Everything okay?" I asked, rather taken aback. Neither of us called one another much while at work unless it was important, let alone received a call from one of his coworkers.

"Now don't get into panic mode. But Mike has been transported to the hospital in an ambulance. They think he had a heart attack." She delivered these words with not much change in her inflection. I suppose she was trying to prevent me from having a meltdown. I wondered if rumor had preceded me, as in my not-so-distant past, I had been characterized as the sovereign ruler of histrionic meltdowns. "He called me from his cell phone from the parking lot," she said, "and told me he could not get out of his car and would I call 911."

"Oh-oh-oh . . . shit," I said as I felt the color leave my face and collect in a slick puddle in my stomach. "He seemed okay this morning when I looked in on him before I went to work. What happened? Oh shit. I'm on my way. Let me tie up some loose ends here. Oh shit."

I got more specifics from her about his symptoms and went in and let my supervisor know. Tears hammered against the back of my eyes, but I gathered them up and threw them somewhere in the corner for later. I jumped into my car as my thoughts spun like a tornado in my head. I instinctively turned on the radio and heard Vince Gill's "High on the Mountain," and I almost started sobbing right then and there. I don't like Country as a rule, but I have a few favorites and this was one of them. I concentrated on my driving. Cars whizzed by. Everything took on that surreal quality I knew so well when the unexpected happens and it affects everything about life. I felt numb and as if every molecule in my body was on fire at the same time.

The hospital loomed in front of me like an enemy from my past whom I didn't want to acknowledge and hoped would not acknowledge me. I tried so hard to be mindful of my emotions and accept where I was, but the more I tried, the more panic seemed to batter me.

Mike was in the emergency room, trying to look like he was not in as much pain as he was in. His eyes had tell-tale signs that he was hurting. The nurse bustled in and gave him some morphine. She kept saying, "He has had a major heart event." She would not commit to whether or not it was a heart attack.

Mike was in a triage room. We waited for hours. Finally, a doctor came in and offered, "We are rotating shifts and are waiting to talk to the cardiologist," as an explanation. We sat in the cramped room, and I watched people being pushed in gurneys back and forth and nurses huddling together as if strategizing the final play in a football game.

I went to get a cup of coffee and made some calls to let friends and family know of his situation. I watched a family gather hands and pray as tears fell from their eyes. My heart did a flip in my chest. I abruptly got up and left half a cup of coffee sitting on the table with year-old magazines no one really read but just absently leafed through to keep their emotions at bay.

Mike was still in pain. They were administering various concoctions, I assumed to alleviate the pain. Periodically, he squeezed my hand. I felt completely powerless. The cardiologist finally arrived and declared Mike had had a heart attack. They wanted to do a "cardiac catheterization" to determine the extent of damage and if a stent was needed.

I went to the assigned waiting room. I sat silently and as still as if in a trance. Someone's voice startled me to my senses, and a hand touched my shoulder. It was my brother.

"Rachel, how is he doing?" Thomas inquired softly with concern filling his eyes.

I started crying as soon as I became consciously aware of him. He sat down beside me and held me as silent tears fell. Not a word was said. I felt a connection so deep and profound I still cannot give it proper words. I was convinced it was spiritual even though I still had a hard time defining what that meant to me. This spiritual feeling was mine, and it was okay if I couldn't define it. Sometimes I wondered if giving feelings and experiences definitions was half my problem. I would then spend long hours analyzing my thoughts about those feelings, comparing and trying to formalize something that was just meant to be felt. Then I would assign values to my definitions and worry about if others thought I was living up to those values. It was comparable to being a fly in a spider web trying to wiggle free.

In between my gasps for air and occasionally renewed attacks of tears, I related the best I could to Thomas what was going on with Mike.

"We had one of our stupid arguments last night. I feel like such a shit, I mean, witch," I said, looking up at him with apologetic eyes of someone who was trying to clean up her language. "Thank goodness I had written him one of my goofy love notes before I left this morning. I love him so much. I don't know what I would do if anything happens to him."

"He is going to be fine," Thomas said. "You are just going to have to quit stressing him out so much!" he wisecracked.

"What . . . oh yeah . . . I guess you are right," I said with a slight giggle. I felt totally supported. Of course, neither of us wanted to sit in our true feelings too very long. Thomas used humor to deflect his feelings and discomfort with my feelings and it seemed to help for short increments. It was okay to allow feelings to pass just as well as allowing myself to feel them. I didn't have to beat them into submission before letting them go.

We sat for hours. Thomas brought his laptop and was immersed in work. I tried to read a book he had bought me, *The Creative Life* by

Julia Cameron, but I could not concentrate on it. Instead, I had a stare down with the clock in the waiting room. Finally, a nurse came in and indicated they had put in a stent and that Mike was already in a room and doing as well as could be expected. They confirmed he had a serious heart attack. He was in and out of consciousness, but responsive when he drifted awake. He smiled when Thomas interjected, "Well, buddy, this is a hell of a way to get me to come see you!"

I spent the night in the surprisingly comfortable recliner next to Mike. A nurse had even brought warmed blankets for me.

The cardiologist came the following day and talked to us about the blockage in the vessels to his heart and the possibility of bypass surgery. In the middle of the doctor's consult, I agonized about my breath and talked out of the side of my mouth, looking like I might have had a stroke when I asked what I thought were pertinent questions. Immediately after the cardiologist left, I used Mike's toothbrush and toothpaste provided by the hospital. I felt sheepish for being obsessed about my breath right after my husband had a heart attack. Funny how little things seem to hold such significance at times of great stress.

The stent had corrected the issues with his coronary artery. He said there had been some discussion with the younger team members whether time and the right medications would allow his heart to heal so he might be able to avoid the more invasive procedure. We both preferred the conservative option. Thomas, who had stayed overnight, said, "Let's hope whatever you do works, because Mike is all heart and would not seem like himself if it weren't working right!"

I looked at him and half-smiled. *What a sap* I thought endearingly.

Joanne, Mike's sister, relieved me so I could swing by the office. Not long after Julia died, Joanne had moved to Key West, Florida, with the coaxing of her best friend who lived there. Joanne took the next flight to Asheville after hearing of Mike's heart attack. It was good to see her. We had always tried to get together for holidays and special events and stayed in touch by texting and Skype, but still, seeing her in person was better. We hugged hard and long. We vowed to visit one another more often "just because." I was self-conscious that I still had not been down to the Keys to visit. She looked rested and happy, even though her brother was in the hospital, and I told her so. She told me she loved her job as manager of a bed-and-breakfast inn, and had "met someone." I knew we would have girl time later, so I did not ask more.

I still had a hard time putting my work aside even at a time of personal crisis. I know that it was distorted thinking, but I was fearful that all my clients' lives would fall apart at the same time if I weren't there doing the work I was hired to do. Even though my head and my support network encouraged me to recite the serenity prayer and take my unrealistic expectations out of the picture, I struggled with this concept. It was hard for me to dig in too deep and look at the fear that still sat ready to leap like a forgotten soul perched on a cliff ready to end it all. My fear was always self-centered at its heart. I was afraid I wouldn't get something I thought I needed or lose something I already had. And since helping others made me feel worthy, I lied to myself, declaring I was irreplaceable, but underneath, I believed I was expendable. That, combined with an honest desire to serve, drove me to almost workaholic standards.

Afterward, I swung by the house to give Satchmo some needed attention and to take him into the woods to run. It was there that I found my solace. Mike was going to be all right. As if he knew about my recent life events, Satchmo licked my face when I sat down at the base of a tree to give silent thanks. I hugged him and talked nonsense to him. Nature always has a way of putting my life in perspective and instilling some sense of humility, gratitude and connectivity. I can't put it into words. A member at one of our meetings, when discussing the necessity of a "spiritual awakening," said that he likened it to something he heard. "There was a monastery where the monk took one of his followers to the river and held his head underwater forcefully for a long period of time. When he allowed him back up, the follower took a huge gulp of air, sputtered and looked wild-eyed. The monk then asked him what he was thinking while he was held underwater. He responded, 'I wanted to breathe.' The monk then said, 'When you want God as much as air, then you will be filled.' I don't know the source of this inspirational story, but I know that nature sometimes helps me empty my mind and be filled.

Mike had to be put on a whole cluster of medication. For someone who hardly ever took over-the-counter remedies, this seemed a stretch. But, he did not complain. At first he seemed forever tired and depressed, which I learned was common after a heart attack. And he bruised easily due to the blood thinner he was on, which made him curse out loud. But after a couple of weeks of that, he started going to more meetings fueled by this recent bout with vulnerability and humility, and got a new sponsor. He was doing step work. Even though he admittedly struggled with the changes he had to make, he seemed more at peace than I had seen him since Julia's death. How he handled it was a source of inspiration if I didn't get in the way. At times, it motivated me to do more work on *my* recovery, but other times, I simply refused. My will was strong and my "monkey chatter" wanted to re-assert itself at certain times. I still was not as self-aware as I needed to be, so I wasn't always attentive to my internal triggers. Triggers sometimes still caused me to "act out." Especially those associated with my past sexual abuse. My reactions were not due to a particular feeling or situation itself, but the *thoughts* I had attached to that particular feeling or situation. Triggers were something I addressed in groups or individually with my clients. We would develop formalized, individual, relapse-prevention plans. I felt like a hypocrite. Like a plumber who never seems to fix her own faucet, I was not always willing to apply these same tools in my own life. But with all the 12 step work I had done, I was becoming acutely aware of my deficits. If I wanted to make any more progress, I was going to have to do the work. And that secretly annoyed me.

I knew I needed to call Debbie. So, instead, I avoided her and just texted her, indicating I was doing all right and asking how she was. I guess I shouldn't have been surprised when I got her phone call.

"So, I am getting a sense you are avoiding me and running from yourself," she said when I answered the call.

I laughed too loudly, followed with, "Naw . . . just been busy. I'm fine." Of course as soon as I said it, I knew she would call me on it. I was already starting to get irritated with her.

"That stands for fucked-up, insecure, neurotic and emotional—" she started, but I cut her off.

"I know, you've told me that a hundred times!" I snapped. The counselor in me knew that when I wanted to avoid those who told me the truth, I might be in trouble.

"Rachel, I'm not going to pry you open like a can of tuna fish. When you want to be honest and talk about your feelings, call me. Until then, you probably need to get your butt to a meeting! I'm here when you are ready to talk."

"Okay . . . okay," I muttered as I hung up.

I stared at the cell phone like it was an alien from outer space. I placed it on the counter and plugged it into the outlet so it could charge up. Then I started wiping down the other counters and even cleaning the kitchen cabinets. Before I could even anticipate my next movements, I had pulled out all sorts of cleaning supplies from the cupboard and started frantically cleaning everything I could think of cleaning. Satchmo followed me around like a calf that wanted its mother's teat.

I stopped in my tracks and fussed at him, "Stop following me around!" I yelled. "Go! Go lie down somewhere!" Satchmo hunkered down as if he were afraid of me. I looked at him and my heart softened.

"Oh, sweetie, I love you! I can be bitchy sometimes, can't I?" I reached and rubbed behind his ears. He forgave me immediately, and I wished I was more like him. Both of us went to my favorite chair, a leather and wood chair that reclined but didn't look like a recliner, but more like a piece of period arts-and-crafts furniture. I picked up my cell phone and called Debbie back. We talked for a couple of hours, and it felt good to be able to identify what I had been bottling up and to share my fears and anxiety.

"I was so afraid that God was going to even the score for all my indiscretions and take Mike away from me. Then, as God's timing had it, right before Mike had his heart attack, I acted like a major ass wipe and embraced my drama like a long-lost child. Sometimes, I get so angry with myself. I feel like I should be farther along on my journey and not still acting like a baby when I am uncomfortable or not getting something I think I want," I rattled on.

"You are where you are. We all regress. The good thing is that you recognize it and try your best to address it. Remember your maintenance steps. Step ten says, 'Continued to take personal inventory and when we were wrong promptly admitted it.' That says to me that we are all human and will still wrong one another, which is the reason for this step." Debbie took a deep breath, which I could hear clearly over the telephone, and continued, "Step eleven says, 'Sought through prayer and meditation to improve our conscious contact with God as we understood Him (or Her), praying only for knowledge of His will for us and the power to carry that out,' which makes me think that we always need guidance and need to act on that need for guidance." At the end of our earnest conversation, we agreed to go to a meeting the following night and for the next three thereafter.

Mike and I agreed to start going to a meeting together again at least one time a week, We also decided to explore faith communities and consider attending one. We agreed that our spiritual life needed to expand, and we couldn't just wish that into existence. It would require some footwork. Together we went on the Internet and researched local churches and faith communities. We agreed we wanted to attend one that was fairly close to where we lived, had a wide age range of members, was pretty liberal and had several volunteer activities and educational classes we might be interested in. We even talked about doing mission work together in another country. Our desire was to do secular mission work in areas of woman empowerment, education and literacy, or child development, which we thought would enhance our spiritual growth. We brought our coffee cups and set them on the desk. We huddled together like birds on a telephone wire as we searched. Satchmo lay at our feet. It was almost sexy. And sometimes it made us get all hot and bothered.

△

Wait for the miracle to happen.
12 step program wisdom

It was a couple of weeks later I got up on a Saturday morning and felt dizzy. Then sick to my stomach. I barely made it to the bathroom when I vomited up whatever was left of my dinner the previous night.

"You okay, babe?" Mike called from the kitchen. He had already started to fry up some bacon, onions and home-grown peppers for an omelet. He made the best omelets: fluffy and light with incredible flavor. I was never quite sure what spices he used, but they accentuated the taste like farm fresh butter and that honey you buy at a roadside market do on hot biscuits fresh from the oven. But this time, the smell just made me even more nauseated.

Satchmo trotted into the bathroom and laid down with a plop right next to where I knelt by the toilet. It reminded me of the times I prayed at this basin in days gone by, promising for the millionth time to quit drinking and drugging.

Mike pushed open the bathroom door and stepped quietly inside, "Can I do anything for you?" he inquired softly.

"No . . . I think I'll just go lie back down." I got up and washed my face and brushed my teeth and crawled back into bed. *I must have a stomach virus,* I thought.

"Mommy doesn't feel good," Mike said to Satchmo. Satchmo jumped up on the bed with me and curled up into the small of my back.

At work Monday it occurred to me I had not had my period. We had been using birth control, but I had sporadically missed a day here and there unintentionally. Even though Mike and I had been in those beginning stages of talking about having children, I wasn't certain that now was a time that was good for us. But another part of me was jumping for joy, clicking my heels together and clapping hands.

After a couple of mornings like the previous Saturday morning, I went to the CVS pharmacy located nearest our house and got a home pregnancy test. I stared at the little blue line for the longest time as if I were a miner who had just found a vein of gold.

I went to Babies R Us and picked out the sweetest little pair of baby shoes I could find and draped them over the front door knob for Mike to see when he got home from work. I thought I was being clever and funny. It was my attempt at street humor in an effort to mimic a gang sign where members throw their tennis shoes over the telephone lines, marking their territory or to pin-point a drug-dealing zone. Urban legend suggested all sorts of reasons that these shoes were strewn over power lines—from crack dealers marking their territory to gang members creating an informal memorial for another member who died at that spot. Mike and I always referred to it as my drug radar. Mike had always been pretty observant of his surroundings, so I knew he would see them.

I heard Mike fumbling with his keys and then heard his keys fall to the ground and him say, "What the . . . oh . . . really . . . Rachel, Rachel . . ."

I ran to the door and opened it, grinning. He had tears in his eyes. Mike casually remarked with a silly edge to his voice, "I thought there were baby 'gang-bangers' inside . . ."

Mike's inane comment caused me to laugh with no reserve until I was doing a little two-step to keep from peeing in my pants. And then Mike started his hoot, and we held each other as urine trickled down my leg.

I continued to have the occasional nausea associated with the first trimester, but it wasn't too bad. Compared to the symptoms of substance withdrawal—such as dry mouth, restless legs, insomnia from my mind racing, cramping and vomiting—it was a ramble around a park lake! Mike was attentive and overly protective, which I found endearing most days. Other days it was annoying, but not to the point I vocalized it. I was learning not to vocalize my negativity unless necessary. Just saying things off the top of my head seemed to add a whole new level of complication and hassle that I no longer wanted to indulge. I was beginning to believe that feelings actually did pass. Satchmo seemed to also know that something was different, or at least I thought he did. He looked as if he were on guard and sat at my feet more often than not wherever I ventured in the house.

My belly started to feel fuller, and I noticed a slight bump starting to form. I put elastic in a couple of my favorite jeans early on, but finally gave in and went with Mike to get some maternity clothes. We started considering how we wanted to arrange the nursery. My tendency to want to "fix things" found an acceptable venue. We debated colors, giving it way more credence than needed. We settled on a soft green that would be perfect for either a boy or a girl. I painted a tree on one wall with all sorts of whimsical forest creatures. I made it a birch tree to honor my Russian father. Mike refinished a crib that had been Julia's when she was a baby. A friend of mine made a one-of-a-kind mobile with a variety of felt owls and birds hanging from it. We found a really rustic rocking chair that was broken, sitting on the side of the road. Together, with hard work and ingenuity, we restored it back to its original glory. We repurposed an old vintage dresser we found in an out-of-the-way resale store in Burnsville, North Carolina, and turned it into a changing table.

Mike was probably more creative than I was in some aspects. He made a built-in window seat that doubled as a toy chest flanked by bookshelves. I made curtains with fun, oversized buttons and made the cushions for the window seat and rocking chair in a complementary fabric. We found an ultra-soft area rug to put on the hand-hewn wood floors. If any dust bunnies had gathered in the corners of this room, they must have scattered in fear, knowing I would devour them for dinner. I realized it was my tendency to be obsessive about decorating and cleanliness. It was something I could control, and that was not something I felt I had experienced much throughout the course of my life. My brother, Thomas, when I was younger, used to come into my room and move my knick-knacks around, or turn them upside down just to be annoying. I always knew what had been moved, and put it back exactly in the place it had been before he disturbed it.

"Hey, not bad for a couple of amateur decorators," I said to Mike. My face beamed like an Olympic athlete after winning first place in his or her competition. Something about using our hands, imagination and talents to transform this plain room into a nursery felt beyond good. It had become a need. I relished any opportunity to take something plain and even broken and transform it into something brand new and useful. This had become a familiar theme in my life, and the results made me proud.

Mike said as an afterthought, "Yeah, you work me like a dog. Work your fingers to the bone and what do you get?"

"Boney Fingers!" we both chimed in and then laughed.

I was getting huge and was amazed at the transformation of my body. I took pride in watching what I ate, although occasionally I would succumb and indulge in York Peppermint Patties and peanut-butter-and-banana milkshakes. I continued to exercise on a regular basis. Mike had bought me an exercise video for pregnant women, and I did the routine every other day and still took Satchmo for long walks daily. When we went in for an ultrasound, we found out why I seemed bigger than big. My Ob-Gyn gelled up my protruding belly for our scheduled sonogram. I strained to look at the screen as she talked out loud. Mike hovered near my shoulder and occasionally massaged my neck.

"Can you see that? There seems to be a party for two going on in your belly . . ." She chuckled. "You are having twins!"

"Where? What? Boys? Girls? Oh, my!" I said as my words seemed to trip on each other.

"Yeah . . . yeah . . . I can see them," Mike said, his voice rising an octave. "Lookie there, Rachel!"

"Well, let's see . . . hmmm . . . that one is a little boy . . . see?" Dr. Lanier said.

"Yeah . . . yeah . . . that's my boy!" Mike said as only a proud father would.

"And this one is . . . a . . . a . . . little girl!" Dr. Lanier added after a pause.

I started crying. Blubbering, actually.

"What's wrong, baby?" Mike asked in a surprisingly fatherly tone.

"We only have one crib!" I said and started crying even harder. Both Dr. Lanier and Mike started laughing, and I realized I was just feeling overwhelmed. After the moment passed, I smiled a crooked smile and asked, "Are they okay?"

"They are just fine, Rachel. They are developing right on target. We might want to monitor you a little more closely, that's all," she replied as if talking to a young child. Of course, I was rolling around in fear like a dog in excrement. One baby seemed a little overwhelming as it was. But two?

"I don't know if I can do this . . . what if I screw them up? What if I don't have the patience needed to tend to them? What if they carry our genes and both become addicts? Oh, geez, what have we done? Are we ready for this?" I almost screamed.

"Baby, baby . . . calm down . . . you will do fine," Mike said soothingly. "WE will do fine. You are not doing this all by yourself. Besides, you are one of the kindest, most caring women I have ever known. You will make a great mother,"

Later that week, as I rubbed my belly and talked to my babies, I thought of my mother and father. I had been thinking of them a lot and had done, with Debbie's support, a thorough 9th step just for them. The 9th step dictated that we "made direct amends" to those persons we had identified in the 8th step whom we had harmed, emphasizing the need for thoughtfulness, courage and "prudence" in order to properly complete it. Even if I could not make direct amends in person to my mother and father, I had become willing to take ownership of my character defects and the part those shortcomings played in my relationship with my parents. Especially with my mother.

Debbie had me write a letter to each of them and then burn it. The weight that I had carried forever and a day slipped off my shoulders as if I had removed football pads.

* * *

I drifted back to a time when I was about seven years old and was in the kitchen with my mother baking cookies. We were making them for Christmas. I could feel the tenderness underneath her words as she instructed me on how to fold in the ingredients, which consisted of an amazing blend of figs and spices. I have been trying to find the recipe ever since. She let me lick the beaters. She loved Burl Ives. She couldn't carry a tune if her life depended on it, but when she was relaxed and happy, she sang. I always joined her. She especially loved Burl Ives' song, "A Little Bitty Tear":

> *A little bitty tear let me down*
> *Spoiled my act as a clown*
> *I had it made up*
> *Not make a frown*
> *But a little bitty tear let me down.*

"You sing like I always wanted to," she said as she stroked my face. And then we sang another song and danced around the room. She grabbed one of the fresh baked cookies we had made and gobbled it whole. These cookies, stuffed with a heavenly fig concoction that would make a Catholic bishop become a glutton, were my favorite. I followed her lead, and with crumbs squatting on our faces, we laughed for no particular reason. It was the kind of laughter that erupts from the deepest parts.

I recalled the oversized *Webster's Dictionary* she kept in the kitchen. She had built a little shelf for it to sit on and always had me look up words I didn't know the meaning of. I kind of hated that as a child because I assumed she was insinuating I was stupid. But on this day, we were laughing so hard that it caused her to collide into the corner of the shelf the dictionary sat on. I know it must have hurt because she pulled up her shirt to examine the bruise that was already forming, but instead of complaining, she just laughed harder.

"I guess if we looked up the word 'clumsy' in the dictionary, my name would appear," she said with a chuckle, "but if we looked up the word for 'talent,' it would be your name."

My mother always seemed an anomaly to me. She wore Wrangler jeans, a Timex watch wound around her belt loop and men's black and white Ked's tennis shoes; she had stylishly attractive short-cropped sensible hair. She was pretty and vibrant but did not seem to want to call attention to that fact. More than anything, she was practical and smart, and if I concentrated really hard, I remembered that she could be spontaneous and very funny. I caught her exaggerated dancing in the kitchen when she thought no one was watching, singing that old Enjoli perfume TV ad campaign portraying superwomen who could, "bring home the bacon, fry it up in a pan and never let you forget you're a man." Born in the fifties, she had to have been pulled by the traditional values of that era when a woman was viewed as an extension of her mate. I interpreted this to mean women were seen as not having as much value in and of themselves.

Then, came the sixties, which attempted to challenge those same values and beliefs and turn them upside down, but, like a stain that has sat on a shirt too long, it is hard to erase that blemish completely. I imagined it made it even harder for her to adopt a new set of values that she actually held as true. It was then, sitting in this memory, that I recognized that she loved me and had always loved me. I had been so consumed with fear and anger that I had blamed her for my sexual abuse. I also believed that who I had or had not become had nothing to do with her, but at the same time, it had everything to do with her. That was the dichotomy of being a parent. I had been convinced for so long that she thought I was what I believed myself to be, defective. It never occurred to me that she had her own fears and sense of inadequacy and just did not have the answers on how to make my hurt go away. So she retreated at times. Even though she never said it out loud in so many words, she had tried to share her heart with me; I started remembering bits and pieces of times she just didn't know any better how to do that than I did.

"I don't get depressed," she stated matter-of-factly when one of many therapists we had been assigned—once the Department of Social Services became involved—spoke to us about the nature of my clinical depression and the *genetic predisposition* associated with it.

"You don't ever feel sad or disheartened?" the counselor asked incuriously.

"No . . . I get angry," Mother said, as if that emotion was more acceptable somehow.

"Do you think that anger could have been masking a deeper feeling of depression or fear?" the therapist asked.

"No! I do not." My mother pulled back and shot her a rubber band of condescending denial.

I remembered Mother telling me once about her father's disappointment that she wasn't a boy, and it all started to make some sense to me. "So I pretended I *was* a boy. I was very convincing," she said, as she pointed to some old photographs she had of herself in an album she took down for us to look at. "All the neighborhood kids thought I was one." She and I were squished together on our couch like marshmallows in a plastic bag that sat out in the car too long. There were several photographs of her in boy's clothes with hair shorn very close to her head. The one I liked best was of her in an Indian costume. I had that one framed after she died. It hangs on the wall going up my stairs. My *wall of fame,* as I call it.

As a child, I was sure my mother, like the entirety of mothers everywhere, should have all the answers. It was her job to fix what was broken in me and love me until I could love myself. She should just intuitively know how to do this. It wasn't fair that she wasn't doing her job that I saw all the other mothers in the world were doing. *She must not love me enough*, I decided. Now that I was getting ready to be a mother, I recognized that this was another lie that I had assimilated as my mantra. I saw her for the first time as separate and human.

I subsequently felt my babies stir inside me. In that brief instant, I was convinced my mother and I did the best we could with what we had to work with. That seething anger I had carried around with me like a knife in a sheath dissipated. Wishing I would have put down my weapon long before she died and feeling the heaviness of grief that lay on my heart, I cried anguished tears for my loss. It was as if I had slipped out of the heels I wore to work and put on my comfortable bedroom slippers. Crying felt freeing. I cried for the loss of my childhood at the hands of *my* monster, "Ollie," the red-headed fiend. I cried that I had indulged myself and become my own monster. I wept for my lost child within. Allowing my tears to fall, not bothering to wipe my nose or judging myself harshly, I just sat in my grief for a long time. It felt right. It felt good. And then I prayed. I gave thanks for new beginnings. I talked to both my mother and father in my prayer and asked them for forgiveness and told them how much I loved them.

As I looked back over the last couple of months, I was astounded as I realized that I no longer was obsessing about using drugs and alcohol to dodge my feelings. I now had started challenging my irrational idea that any negative feelings would swallow me and spit me out and I would crumble into a useless heap of skin and bones, unable to move or produce. I had been persuaded, due to the changes I had made in my life, and the sincere program I actually was trying to incorporate into my daily living, that I could walk through pain and maybe, just maybe, come out the other side. Yes, the thought of using might pass through my addled brain at times, but I knew it just wasn't an option and automatically dismissed it. *This was a first.* I said out loud, "I wish you guys would get to meet your grandparents. I know they are keeping guard AND probably laughing, knowing what the road ahead looks like."

When Mike came home that evening, we snuggled on the couch, and I shared my memories with him while Satchmo gnawed on a rawhide bone. Mike listened attentively and caressed my shoulders when I said, "I want our little man's first name to be Nicholas after my father . . . you can pick the middle name. And I think we should call our daughter Julianne Maija. Anne was my mother's middle name."

Without hesitation, Mike responded with a slight catch in his voice, "Of course . . . that is perfect." I looked down at my lap. Satchmo had managed to squeeze his head and shoulders in between my knees and was looking at me with those earnest, milk chocolate eyes, as if to say, "I always knew things would turn out okay." *And I believed it to be true.*

Afterword

There were times before I gave birth to my beautiful twins and many times afterwards that I questioned my abiding faith and faltered on my commitment to living my life based on the principals of the 12 step program, which had become like my church. I am human.

It takes too much effort, I told myself when I felt overwhelmed by motherhood, holding down a job and life. But I knew resentment was a feeling I would be ill-advised to hold on to. Intuitively, I wanted to be a good example for my children and I wanted to live a life of dignity and grace and just be happy for God's sake. That required setting an intention on a daily basis, sometimes on an hourly basis. But the more I practiced it, the easier it was to want it.

* * *

I thought about my father. My father used to tell me a story, when I was younger, about a Russian monk Rasputin. My father loved Russian history. One of the first books that he and my mother insisted I read was about Nicholas and Alexandra, the Russian czar and his wife. Alexandra, Nicholas's wife, became obsessed with Rasputin, whom she was convinced was a holy man who possessed healing powers. Father said, "Rasputin laid his hands on the czar's son, who suffered from hemophilia, and it was Rasputin's healing powers that caused him to get better. This ability to heal was hard to prove or disprove. But rumors sometimes create legends. Therefore, Rasputin was perceived by many to possess certain, unexplained spiritual powers. It was debated whether they were evil or ordained.

I have since researched Rasputin a little. Like many spiritually focused Russians during that period in time, he believed that salvation depended less on the church than on seeking the spirit of God within. That is similar to my own belief system, but that is as far as it goes. Rasputin also maintained that sin and repentance were interdependent and necessary to salvation. I figured that was a way he rationalized his behavior to himself, the same way I had rationalized my own addictive behavior in days past. He held the delusional belief that yielding to temptation—alcohol and sex—was a necessary evil for the purpose of humiliation and as a means to dispel the sin of vanity. It was a prerequisite needed to proceed to repentance and salvation. Actually, I thought it was poppycock and just a way for him to deceive himself.

Rasputin's reputation became soiled because of his continued debauchery and its perceived negative effect on the Russian monastery. He was brutally murdered—just like an addict whose ends are jails, institutions or death!

This story of Rasputin was another my father related to me sometimes when I was a child. It wasn't clear if he did so out of fascination and his own struggles with spirituality or as a way to keep me in line somehow. Still, I remembered my father, in a tone of utter exasperation and formality that he would adopt when particularly frustrated with me, saying, "Rachel, this life of debauchery that you are choosing to embark upon is going to be your undoing."

Recovery is a program of action. Unlike Rasputin, my indulging in my old behaviors—expecting improved results, expecting to somehow be catapulted in to a spiritual realm—would be insane. I had to embark upon a new way of thinking *and* behaving.

* * *

Often, I am asked, "What led you to recovery?" or "How did you recover?" I think, unless you are an addict, you don't really understand completely the concept that addiction is a brain disease. The symptoms of this disease include obsessive thinking, compulsions, the phenomenon of craving, rationalization, minimization and intellectualization. It is hard for me to explain what goes on in my mind. I am prone to racing thoughts still, but after learning how to manage my illnesses, both depression and addiction, I know that I have to be gentle with myself and accept that I will never be cured and I will always be recovering. And that certainly beats the other alternatives: jails, institutions or death. Many of us who are in recovery insist we are blessed. We have a spiritual program that helps us be our best versions of ourselves, live our lives according to our value systems as best we can (instead of believing one way and living another, which tends to leave a huge gaping hole in the gut), having meaningful relationships and understanding the concept of pure joy vs. maniacal laughter while under the influence.

Again, though, how did I recover? I have often asked myself that as I have watched many of us relapse—even those I thought never would—and watch them lose everything they hold dear, including their sanity and many times their lives.

My mind, even in recovery, still wants to reach back into my past and pick at strands of shame that still cleave my heart. It is just not as often now nor as long when it does happen. And now I have means to deal with these random thoughts that I never had before. As they say in recovery, not only are my feelings not facts, but sometimes the thoughts associated with these feelings are not facts either. There is much emphasis in recovery circles about how the past may have carved out some of my personality and belief system, but today, I don't have to live there. Most days, I am able to stay focused on today and what I can do today about tomorrow. And not only do I try and enjoy the day, but my tomorrow seems hopeful. When I was in active addiction, nothing seemed hopeful. Hope was sucked out of me like ear wax in a rubber syringe. I had to use substances just so I wouldn't kill myself. Hope and purpose are two reasons for living and I was devoid of them.

I am also insightful enough to know my triggers, which usually are unpleasant memories made to seem desirable, memories that sometimes come out of nowhere—like a storm cloud in a clear blue sky—trying to get me to pick back up. For some reason, my addiction will latch on to these recollections and try to twist them around to make them appear desirable to recreate. My sponsor, Debbie, calls them "blasts from the past" that you don't want to indulge. In my early recovery, I fed them, and like sharks in the ocean, they would multiply. Now, as soon as they rev up, I will acknowledge them and then very quickly either distract myself or call them out as the great deceivers that they are . . . and tell on my disease to someone in recovery.

The truth of the matter is, I love recovery and who I have become, and now I am willing to do whatever I need to do to stay in recovery. That is the HOW of recovery, some say—being honest, open-minded and willing.

So, I guess I attribute my recovery to: 1) a spiritual awakening, which I cannot define or understand; 2) people believing in me, especially Maija in the beginning and later on, my sponsor; 3) my recovery network (even strangers like the bartender in the bar); 4) service work, including working with others in the 12 step rooms; 5) my profession, which lends itself to a living reminder of who I am; 6) picking up and using the tools that I have learned (going to meetings, recognizing my own triggers that make me think of using, getting a sponsor, reading the literature and applying the steps in all my daily interactions as best I can; 7) and accepting that addiction is a disease and I have it.

So with that new belief system engraved in both my head and heart, I move through each day. And each day is exactly what it is supposed to be.

* * *

Mike and I are content with our life. We are not giddy and happy every day. We are not worried and depressed every other day. Life is not like that. I have found that if I obsess about how I will feel tomorrow, and if I will be able to handle tomorrow, then I lose today. And today is a precious commodity. Today, I hear my twins babbling, and I hear gurgling laughter escape from their throats like bubbles in soda pop when Satchmo plays with them. Today, I see tears form in Mike's eyes as an expression of love as he watches them play. Today, I see God in everything, even grief, if I look closely. And that is enough.